BRIAN
ALDISS

Starmont Reader's Guide 28

MICHAEL R. COLLINGS

Series Editor: Roger C. Schlobin

Starmont House
Mercer Island, Washington
1986

Acknowledgments and Dedication

To Brian and Margaret Aldiss, for their unfailing interest and support;
To Roger Schlobin and Ted Dikty, for their commitment to the Starmont Series;
To David Engebretson, for his assistance in research;
To the Huntington Library, for making their collection of Aldiss letters available;
To the editors at Atheneum, for sharing the Helliconia materials;
And always, to Judith, for encouraging me and making it possible to complete this study.

—Thousand Oaks, CA
January 1985

Published and copyright © 1986 by Starmont House, Inc., P. O. Box 851, Mercer Island, WA 98040. All rights reserved. International copyrights reserved in all countries. No part of this book may be reproduced in any form, except for brief passages quoted in reviews, without the expressed written permission of the publisher.

Cover design by Stephen E. Fabian.

Printed In U.S.A.

First Edition — February 1986

Library of Congress Cataloging-in-Publication Data

Collings, Michael R.
    Brian W. Aldiss.

    (Starmont reader's guide ; 28)
    Bibliography: p.
    Includes index.
    1. Aldiss, Brian Wilson, 1925–   —Criticism and interpretation.   2. Science fiction, English—History and criticism.   I. Title.   II. Series.
PR6051.L3Z6   1986   823'.914   85-17224
ISBN 0-916732-99-1
ISBN 0-916732-74-6 (pbk.)

MICHAEL R. COLLINGS is an Associate Professor of English at Pepperdine University in Malibu, CA. His earlier volume in the Starmont Reader's Guide Series, *Piers Anthony*, was published in November 1983.

CONTENTS

Abbreviations

BYS	*Billion Year Spree*
DLY	*Dark Light Years*
EMH	*The Eighty-Minute Hour*
ES	*Enemies of the System*
FrU	*Frankenstein Unbound*
LW	*Life in the West*
MOI	*Moreau's Other Island (An Island Called Moreau)*
MT	*The Malacia Tapestry*
RPA	*Report on Probability A*
STAN	*Space, Time, and Nathaniel*

I
Canon and Chronology

1925   Born August 18, 1925. East Dereham, Norfolk, England, to Stanley Aldiss (outfitter) and Elizabeth May Wilson

1939-42   Attended West Buckland School

1943-47   Served in Royal Corps of Signals, Far East (attached to Indian Army, 1945-1946)

1947   Began career as bookseller in Oxford (until 1956)

1953   Published "Now Consolidate"

1954   First professional sale, "A Book in Time," in *The Bookseller*.[1] First science-fiction story, "Criminal Record," in *Science Fantasy*.

1955   Birth of first child, Clive. *The Brightfount Diaries* (non-SF novel)

1957   Literary Editor, *Oxford Mail* (to 1969). *Space, Time, and Nathaniel* (coll)

1958   Special Plaque, Sixteenth World Science Fiction (Solacon) as Most Promising New Author of the Year. *Non-Stop* (retitled *Starship*)

1959   Birth of second child, Caroline Wendy. Received World Science Fiction Convention Citation. *Starship* (see *Non-Stop* [1958]); *Vanguard From Alpha; No Time Like Tomorrow* (coll); *The Canopy of Time* (coll)

1960   President, British Science Fiction Association, 1960-1964. *Bow Down to Nul* (retitled *The Interpreter*); *Galaxies Like Grains of Sand* (coll)

1961   Editor, Penguin Science-Fiction Series (1961-1964). *The Interpreter* (see *Bow Down to Nul* [1960]); *The Primal Urge; The Male Response; Penguin Science Fiction* (anth); *Equator* (coll)

1962   Received Hugo Award for *Hothouse*. *Hothouse* (retitled *Long Afternoon of Earth*); *Best Fantasy Stories* (anth)

1963   Invited Guest, First Festival Internazionale del Film di Fantascienze (Trieste). *More Penguin Science Fiction* (anth): *The Airs of Earth* (coll)

1964   Co-edited *SF Horizons* (1964-1965). *Greybeard; The Dark Light Years; Starswarm* (coll); *Introducing SF* (anth); *Yet More Penguin Science Fiction* (anth)

1965   Married (second wife) Margaret Christine Manson, 11 December 1965. Received Nebula Award for "The Saliva Tree."

1

Guest of Honor, 23rd World Science Fiction Convention ("Loncon"). *Earthworks; Best Science Fiction Stories of Brian W. Aldiss* (coll); retitled *Who Can Replace a Man?*

1966   Invited Guest, Nebula Awards, New York. *The Saliva Tree and Other Strange Growths* (coll); *Who Can Replace a Man?* (coll; see *Best Science Fiction Stories of Brian W. Aldiss* [1965]); *Cities and Stones: A Traveller's Guide to Yugoslavia* (nonf)

1967   Birth of third child, Timothy Nicholas. Began editing *Best SF* series with Harry Harrison, retitled *The Year's Best Science Fiction* in England (to 1975). *An Age* (retitled *Cryptozoic!*); *Nebula Award Stories Two* (anth; with Harry Harrison)

1968   *Cryptozoic!* (see *An Age* [1967]); *Report on Probability A; Farewell, Fantastic Venus* (anth; with Harry Harrison; retitled *All About Venus*)

1969   Birth of fourth child, Charlotte May. "Most Popular British Science Fiction Writer," British Science Fiction Association. In a letter to Larry Ashmead Aldiss wrote:

> ". . . I've just been voted Britain's most popular SF writer. . . . Of course I'm pleased, but it's rather funny, really, since I'm slowly working away from the field—or rather, more centrally in to what I feel sf should be about."[2]

Invited Guest, SF Symposium, International Film Festival, Rio de Janeiro. *Barefoot in the Head; Intangibles, Inc., and Other Stories* (coll); *A Brian Aldiss Omnibus* (coll; includes *The Interpreter, The Primal Urge,* and selected stories)

1970   Ditmar Award (Australia), "Most Popular Contemporary Science Fiction Writer." Invited Guest, First International Science Fiction Symposium (Tokyo). *Neanderthal Planet* (coll); *The Moment of Eclipse* (coll); *The Hand-Reared Boy* (non-SF); *The Shape of Further Things: Speculations on Change* (nonf)

1971   *A Soldier Erect: or, The Further Adventures of the Hand-Reared Boy* (non-SF novel); *Brian Aldiss Omnibus 2* (coll; includes *Space, Time, and Nathaniel; Non-Stop; The Male Response*); *Best Science Fiction Stories of Brian W. Aldiss* (coll; revised)

1972   BSFA Award, for *The Moment of Eclipse.* Co-Founder John W. Campbell Memorial Award. *The Astounding-Analog Reader, Vol. I* (anth; with Harry Harrison); *The Book of Brian Aldiss* (coll; retitled *The Comic Inferno*)

1973   *Frankenstein Unbound; The Comic Inferno* (coll; see *The Book of Brian Aldiss* [1972]); *The Astounding-Analog Reader, Vol. II* (anth; with Harry Harrison); *The Penguin*

	Science Fiction Omnibus (anth; contains *Penguin Science Fiction, More Penguin Science Fiction, Yet More Penguin Science Fiction*); *Billion Year Spree: The True History of Science Fiction* (nonf)
1974	BSFA special award. *The Eighty-Minute Hour; Space Opera* (anth)
1975	Guest of Honor, Lunacon, New York. Co-President, Eurocon (1975-1979), Vice-President, Stapledon Society. *Space Odysseys* (anth); *Decade the 1940s; Science Fiction Art* (nonf); *Hell's Cartographers* (nonf)
1976	Chairman, John W. Campbell Memorial Award (1976-1978). Eurocon Award. *The Malacia Tapestry; Decade the 1950s* (anth); *Galactic Empires, Vol. 1* (anth); *Galactic Empires, Vol. II* (anth)
1977	James Blish Award (for non-fiction). Cometa d'Argento, Italy. Prix Jules Verne. Founding Trustee, World Science Fiction, Dublin. *Last Orders and Other Stories* (coll); *Decade the 1960s* (anth; with Harry Harrison)
1978	Pilgrim Award, Science Fiction Research Association. Chairman, Society of Authors, London (1978-1979). Member, Arts Council Literature Panel (1978-1980). *Brothers of the Head; Enemies of the System; A Rude Awakening* (non-SF); *Perilous Planets* (anth)
1979	Guest of Honor, World Science Fiction Convention. *Pile: Petals from St Klaed's Computer* (poetry); *New Arrivals, Old Encounters* (coll); *Evil Earths* (anth)
1980	*Moreau's Other Island* (retitled *An Island Called Moreau*); *Life in the West* (non-SF)
1981	*An Island Called Moreau* (see *Moreau's Other Island* [1981]); *Foreign Bodies* (coll); *This World and Nearer Ones: Essays Exploring the Familiar* (nonf)
1982	Nebula Nomination, *Helliconia Spring. Helliconia Spring; Farewell to a Child* (poetry)
1983	John W. Campbell Memorial Award, *Helliconia Spring.* Special Guest, Fourth International Conference on the Fantastic in the Arts, Boca Raton, FL. *Helliconia Summer; Best of Aldiss* (magazine coll)
1984	Special Guest, Fifth International Conference on the Fantastic in the Arts, Boca Raton, FL. *Seasons in Flight* (coll)
1985	*Helliconia Winter; The Pale Shadow of Science: Recent Essays*

Notes

[1] Because Aldiss has written a large number of short stories, I will not include individual titles in this chronology, unless the short story represents an important moment in his career, e.g., an award-winning story. Many of his stories are included in collections, which are listed; other stories will appear in the bibliography at the end of this volume.

[2] Letter to Larry Ashmead, 22 Nov. 1968. Huntington Library, San Marino, CA.

II
Brian W. Aldiss—Cartographer[1]

Harry Harrison's dedication in *Bill, The Galactic Hero,*

For my shipmate
BRIAN W. ALDISS
who is reading the sextant
and plotting the course
for us all

effectively introduces Aldiss' work. If science fiction aims at "a particular and piercing kind of mimesis because science itself, with all its indeterminacy, seems to be our most ambitious attempt to imitate or map the way things are,"[2] Brian Aldiss is among the most accomplished of mapmakers. Critics have suggested several categories for Aldiss' novels. Richard Mathews, for example, emphasizes the classical imagery of Proteus and Prometheus; Bruce Gillespie sees the pilgrimage as Aldiss' central theme.[3] To consider Aldiss as mapmaker seems more satisfying than either of these, however, since maps relate to landscape by reducing complexities to accessible signs and symbols. They do not reproduce surface characteristics in their entirety, concentrating instead on those which allow subsequent travelers to investigate new territories more efficiently. This is precisely what Aldiss does. True, he suggests Prometheus, a forerunner, by introducing new themes and ideas. And he is a Proteus, stimulating mental adaptation by presenting his readers with science-fictional images and forcing them to adjust their conceptions of humanity, of their place in the universe, and of the universe itself. But beyond that, he defines new territories; he is, in a word, a mapmaker.

Images of mapmaking occur throughout his writing. In *Billion Year Spree* (1973), for example, Aldiss defines science fiction, after first stipulating that "Definitions should be like maps; they help you explore the grounds; they are not substitutes for exploration" (Ch. 1). Earlier, in a 1964 conversation with C. S. Lewis and Kingsley Amis, he explicitly relates a sense of exploration and investigation to his purposes in writing:

> I find I would much rather write science fiction than anything else. The dead weight is so much less there than in the field of the ordinary novel. There's a sense in which you're conquering a fresh country.[4]

4

For Aldiss, science fiction explores the possibilities of space, time, and humanity. He does not substitute for the discoverer and conquerer (there is only a "sense" in which the two overlap); he does not create power-fantasies complete with heroes who can rescue universes; nor does he offer easy entry into alien worlds. Instead, he draws maps, provides human guides—common, ordinary men and women, less than superhuman, who must understand change beyond their abilities to adapt. Through these characters, readers may follow Aldiss' guidelines as he penetrates the convoluted "inwardness" and "outwardness" of humanity (to borrow his terms from *BYS*).

Beginning with his first published science-fiction story, "Criminal Record" (1954), Aldiss provides maps. These are sketches of futures which characters and reader must interpret to understand their own natures. "Impossible Star" (1963) incorporates this image in the character Wilson, described as a celestial mapmaker. "Tyrant's Territory" (1967) concerns efforts to map new territory, both physical and psychological. This sense of the short stories as maps is enhanced in several of the later "Enigmas," sequences of three interwoven and frequently incomplete narratives, which often more suggest stories that might be told than are fully told.

We see the same focus in the novels. *Non-Stop* is an exercise in mapping. Characters penetrate passages within their world to discover that they inhabit a closed spaceship. Ultimately, the map breaks down: the ship disintegrates, and the inhabitants must rejoin humanity. Significantly, the guide-priest's name, Marapper, is almost an anagram for "mapper."

In *Earthworks* Aldiss again maps humanity. Characters move across the devastated landscapes of England, onto the seas, and finally into the deserts of Africa, discovering the boundaries humanity has imposed upon itself. Aldiss suggests the importance of maps by naming a character Peter Mercator. On an earth destroyed by pollution, overcrowding, and human apathy, Mercator's "projection" is to re-draw the maps of human society by starting a nuclear war. Following Mercator's map, the hero can take the first steps toward rescuing humanity from a cesspool-Earth of its own making.

In later novels, Aldiss' maps take on new, more frightening dimensions. "In simpler early structures, like *Non-Stop* and *Hot House*," he has written, "the whole picture or map finally emerges." In later works, "vital clues have already been lost, orientation must remain incomplete because the new perceptual framework had yet to emerge."[5] Thus *Report on Probability A, Barefoot in the Head,* and *An Age* provide new guidelines to meet the requirements of their subjects: objectivity, subjectivity, and the ambiguities of time. *The Malacia Tapestry* carries the process of mapmaking to a logical extreme, as the image of the tapestry supplants the city itself—a static representation of life reduces change and action to only symbol. *Moreau's Other Island* begins with a map left by an earlier ex-

5

plorer, H. G. Wells, then ventures further into the unknown, leaving new signs and symbols to help readers penetrate darkness.[6] The Helliconia novels, with their emphatic sweep across continually changing landscapes, map characters' attempts to understand the contradictions of stasis and change. In these later novels, Aldiss notes, readers may again determine the full dimensions of the map: "by the time of *Malacia* and *Helliconia* . . . the middle-period complexity remains, but again it is possible to conceive of a reliable map. Indeed, Helliconia actually provides a map, physically."[7]

Throughout the novels, we discover the increasingly sophisticated and convoluted touch of Aldiss as mapmaker and guide. "My successful novels," he states, "present territories of the psyche (i.e., in some respect symbolist landscapes), to which the presiding spirit, the writer/reader, must create his own key or map or else perish; it is the necessity rather than the map which presents itself most pressingly to me."[8] Reading Aldiss, we are continually impressed with his fervor, the breathless anxiety for humanity's survival that forms such narratives as *Greybeard, Hothouse, Frankenstein Unbound*, or Helliconia. Aldiss may create maps, but they are not exclusively for pleasure journeys. They lead ultimately to his concern for survival.

Aldiss' criticism, both formal and personal, shows the same concern for mapping. In 1974, Kingsley Amis published *New Maps of Hell*, a work to which Aldiss made tangential reference in his own *Hell's Cartographers*. In the latter, Aldiss argues that science fiction

. . . is not a matter of prediction, and never has been, although prediction is one of the ingredients which makes it fun. Rather it mirrors the present in such a way as to dispense with inessentials and dramatize new trends.[9]

In other words, science fiction reduces complexities and surface convolutions to recognizable symbols and uses those symbols to construct guidelines for readers. Later in the discussion, Aldiss blends the image of mapmaker with that of science-fiction writers as "weather men flying above alien cities, and we have not delivered our reports."[10] There is a feeling of hesitation to make claims too sweeping, coupled with a desire to allow the readers who follow to assume much of the burden of interpretation and understanding.

To read Aldiss' stories, novels, and criticism as maps rather than as escapism, prophecy, or dogma makes them more individual, more compelling, and more meaningful. Aldiss' themes emerge clearly through his maps: chaos and order; inwardness and outwardness; ecological disaster; and inversions of standard and often stereotypic elements of SF, such as the Galactic Empire (as in *Bow Down to Nul*) or space opera (as in *The Eighty-Minute Hour*). His stylistic experiments are equally critical, as in *Barefoot in the Head*, with its evocation of Joycean prose and elliptical poetry, or *Report on Probability A*, with its layers upon layers of cold

6

objectivity, both in plot and in prose. He is, as his various and varied works suggests, one of the few science-fiction writers capable of changing his style with each novel. He has his share of cosmic themes, such as the need for humanity to retain contact with itself; *The Dark Light Years,* for example, is not simply a novel "all about shit" as Harlan Ellison once remarked, but rather a study of humanity's need to integrate rather than divide.[11] Yet rarely does Aldiss present a rigid program for change. Rarely does he sound his voice as one "crying in the wilderness." Instead, he presents maps, guidelines, and suggestions of terrains we might yet encounter and through which we may need help in passing. And, not coincidentally, along the way, he builds bridges between science fiction and mainstream fiction,[12] providing connections not only for himself but for his readers. He is self-admittedly a guide, constantly shifting his focus, refusing to spend too much time with any particular landscape. Colin Greenland concludes that

> . . . the irreducible variety of Aldiss' work is not only the exercise of an agile and energetic mind, but also the expression of a broad and deep imagination which considers it dangerous to look from any viewpoint, even the human one, exclusively. "With every novel," [Aldiss says], "I write, I grasp something, and then don't wish to repeat it; there's always something else to do."[13]

Aldiss makes maps, but given his attitude toward guides and maps, that is a weighty responsibility, which he has met with great dedication for the past three decades.

Notes

[1] An earlier version of this paper was presented to the Fifth International Conference on the Fantastic in the Arts, Boca Raton, FL, 24 March 1984.

[2] Donald M. Hassler, *Comic Tones in Science Fiction* (Westport, CT: Greenwood, 1982), p. 68.

[3] Richard Mathews, *Aldiss Unbound: The Science Fiction of Brian W. Aldiss* (San Bernardino, CA: Borgo, 1977); Bruce Gillespie, "Literature Which Awakens Us: The Science Fiction Novels of Brian W. Aldiss," in *Stellar Gauge: Essays on Modern Science Fiction Writers,* ed. Michael J. Tolley and Kirpal Singh (Melbourne, Australia: Norstrilia, 1980).

[4] "C. S. Lewis Discusses Science Fiction with Kingsley Amis," *SF Horizons* (Spring 1964), p. 11. It is interesting to note the cartographical pun implicit in Lewis' title for the piece, which was reprinted in his *Of Other Worlds* (New York: Macmillan, 1966) as "Unreal Estates."

[5] Letter to Michael R. Collings, 6 April 1984.

[6] He performed a similar experiment somewhat more successfully in the earlier *Frankenstein Unbound,* a novel based on Mary Shelley's *Frankenstein.* Both of Aldiss' novels were written within a year or so of each other, but through a series of circumstances, *Moreau* was not published until 1980.

[7] Letter to Michael R. Collings, 6 April 1984.

[8] Letter to Michael R. Collings, 6 April 1984.

[9] *Hell's Cartographers* (New York: Harper & Row, 1975), 2-3.

[10] *Hell's Cartographers*, p. 3.

[11] Harlan Ellison, *Dangerous Visions* (Garden City, NY: Doubleday, n.d. [Book Club Edition]), 155.

[12] This is the prevailing critical perspective in Brian Griffin and David Wingrove's *Apertures: A Study of the Writings of Brian W. Aldiss* (Westport, CT: Greenwood, 1983).

[13] *The Entropy Exhibition* (London: Routledge & Kegan Paul, 1983), p. 84.

III

Decade the 1950s:
Non-Stop

In 1958, Aldiss published his first science-fiction novel, *Non-Stop*.[1] Responses to it ranged from Robert Conquest's comment that Aldiss' "village of dwarfs inching its way continually forward through the endless decks of 'ponic jungle is brilliantly done"[2] to the *London Times'* "It's a pity about Mr. Aldiss' *Non-Stop.*"[3] Other readers noted similarities between Aldiss' novel and Heinlein's *Orphans in the Sky,* concluding with H. H. Holmes that Aldiss "develops his psychological themes well, tells a good adventure story and holds a few surprises up his sleeve: but the book suffers from the lassitude of a thrice-told tale."[4] Yet neither Heinlein nor Aldiss disguised their spaceship-worlds; in fact, the title of Aldiss' American edition, *Starship*, gives the secret away.[5] *Non-Stop* begins in an overtly mechanical world, at odds with the organic, barbaric jungle setting and primitive social structures of the Greene tribe. The first sentence compares Roy Complain's pulse to radar. Three paragraphs later, men play a game on a board "painted on the deck." And a few pages later, "'ponics'" (a short-hand version of *hydroponics*) form a root system like steel mesh. These images of technology and metallurgy suggest from the beginning that the world in question is an artifact, a ship.

Aldiss' purposes are not the same as Heinlein's. The discovery that the world is a ship is not the great revelation of the novel. Complain's guide, the priest Marapper, already knows that, although he has difficulty convincing others and is himself vague as to what exists "outside." In addition, later definitions of words such as *quarters* and *forwards* relate directly to shipboard language. If Aldiss' purpose was to trace characters as they discover the nature of their world, the change in titles would have indeed been devastating.

The simple trick of locale, however, is not all there is to the novel. *Non-Stop* is the better title since the critical discovery is that the ship is long overdue to arrive at Earth—that it is literally traveling non-stop through space. Aldiss' original title directs the readers' attention toward essential points of development, avoiding potential irrelevancies while presenting an analogy to humanity's own voyage through space. The Earth is a closed system: humanity is as ignorant of its future and destination as Aldiss' characters. The novel becomes a political fable directing readers not toward

... the immensities of interstellar space, but rather back to the human intentions underlying the ghastly paternalism which was responsible for the incarceration, over so many generations, of the descendants of the original crew.[6]

Non-Stop expresses the "inward" rather than the "outward"; it maps human potential, both for the "normal" humans manipulating the imprisoned crew and for the crew itself.

In this sense, *Non-Stop* suggests one of the most ambitious treatments of humanity traveling "non-stop" through its universe, Olaf Stapledon's *Last and First Men*. Like Stapledon, Aldiss anatomizes humanity—its strengths and weaknesses, limits and potentials—through the metaphor of a species moving through space. Humanity alters and modifies to meet environmental and social changes, newly manifesting what is ultimately human divorced from accidents to form and structure. Indeed, Stapledon might have contributed in part to *Non-Stop*; his Fifth Men on Venus suffer a "new and inexplicable decay of the digestive organs" that threatens them with extinction. The disease progresses without cure, even though the cause is discovered to be rare "molecular groupings" in the Venusian atmosphere:

> Education became superficial and limited. Contact with the past was no longer possible. Art lost its significance, and philosophy its dominion over the minds of men. Even applied science began to be too difficult. Unskilled control of the subatomic sources of power led to a number of disasters, which finally gave rise to a superstition that all "tampering with nature" was wicked, and all ancient wisdom a snare of Man's Enemy. Books, instruments, all the treasures of human culture, were therefore burnt. Only the perdurable buildings resisted destruction.[7]

This passage, quoted from Aldiss' *Farewell, Fantastic Venus*, could well summarize *Non-Stop* itself.[8]

Non-Stop is not merely derivative, however, borrowing its narrative form from Heinlein and its scope from Stapledon. It is a complex structure of themes and treatments. In spite of similarities to Heinlein's novel, *Non-Stop* is initially far more complex. In Heinlein, the reader knows that the world is a ship and that he will be reading an adventure. In Aldiss, however, the reader must reconcile two carefully juxtaposed conceptual frameworks; the reader, Jameson notes, is prepared to explore " ... through style, the properties of a peculiar and fascinating world."[9]

But that expectation is unfulfilled; section I of the novel is indeed a jungle adventure, as Complain, Marapper, and others leave their village for the 'ponic jungle, searching for meaning in a world without apparent meaning. By the end of that section, though, Aldiss moves into a "tale of cognition," which concentrates on solving problems. At times, as in the episode describing sentient rats, the novel approaches the fantastic. Section III again subverts expectations, shifting into a "collective catastrophe" tale, as humans join to battle Outsiders, Giants, and armies of rats. Section IV becomes an apocalyptic climax—all elements, even the fantastical ones —are reabsorbed into the science-fictional frame and the novel concludes as a political fable of human manipulative impulses.[10] Jameson argues that the novel continually raises expectations—rather like Delaney's "reading protocols"[11] —then undercuts them. "It seems no accident," Jameson concludes,

> . . . that the fundamental social issues in a book in which the author toys with the reader, constantly shifting direction, baffling the latter's expectation, issuing false generic clues, and in general using his official plot as a pretext for the manipulation of the reader's reactions, should be the problem of the manipulation of man by other men.[12]

Theme is a complex problem, particularly in a novel that shifts generic directions so frequently. The most overt theme, of course, is that of humans trapped in a space-ship world and their subsequent entropic degeneration. Humans have declined, literally and metaphorically becoming smaller, almost accidental in the structure of the ship-world. Society has disintegrated;[13] familial relationships have virtually ceased, children and mother becoming almost strangers by the time the child is "waist high" (I:3). There is no mention of the father. "One of the strongest taboos," the novel continues, "was directed against one man's looking another straight in the eyes: honest, well-intentioned men gave each other only side glances" (I:4). Later, humanity is specifically defined as being on the same scale as the rats.

There is, in addition, little sense of maturity. Immaturity is ritualized and formalized. Proverbs emphasize irrationality: "Leap before you look" (II:1), since the nerves must be the arbiter: "mind was not trustworthy" (II:4). Anti-intellectualism infects virtually everyone in the ship, until passions become accepted responses. Characters retreat into the "customary genuflection of rage" (I:2) and excessive emotional outbursts in the presence of death, while in the climactic final pages, the entire society vents its fears and frustrations in a destructive outburst of unthinking violence.

The deeper problem that *Non-Stop* probes, however, is whether the overtly immature "dizzies" differ from the non-mutated humans observing and controlling them. Aldiss frequently suggests analogues between his social construct and human society. After watching the sentient rats and their treatment of a captive telepathic rabbit, Complain draws parallels between animal and human: both work to survive, giving little thought to larger issues, and Complain "could only say the same of himself until now" (II:4). And the reader can only say the same of humanity . . . until now.

The relation between Aldiss' spaceship-world and human society becomes explicit later, as Complain reads an entry in his ancestor's journal:

Earth! I pray that men's hearts have changed, grown less like the hard metals they have loved and served so long. Nothing but the full flowering of a technological age, such as the Twenty-fourth Century knew, could have launched this miraculous ship; yet the miracle is sterile, cruel. Only a technological age could condemn unborn generations to exist in it, as if man were mere protoplasm, without emotion or aspiration. (III:3)

The ship's creation and final disintegration result from humanity's ingrained sense of destruction. Those who built the vessel and abandoned it and its crew to space; those among the crew who hate and fear it and eventually rip it apart, unconscious of the dangers to themselves; even those who observe and manipulate the crew—all are finally human and share this trait. Complain is the catalyst; his yearning for "the Big Something" compels action. He discovers what he seeks but in the process destroys his world.

The rather conventional narrative of humans imprisoned within a spaceship world supports Aldiss' analysis of society and culture, his concern for the "spectacle of the artificial formation of a culture within the closed situation of the lost ship."[14] The novel satirizes both the objectivity of the scientists on Earth who allow generations of "dizzies" to suffer and the paternalistic politics that Aldiss knew well and satirized in other works. In spite of such science-fictional apparatus as alien proteins, mutated humans, telepathic animals, and spaceships, *Non-Stop* is thematically tied to earth and as such becomes a parable of the human condition. His characters define the physical world of their ship and the psychological world of the readers (II:1). Often the analogies occur in dialogue, giving the novel a sense of double purpose, as when Tregonnin says that

In the days before the first Governor came the catastrophe—whatever that was—and since then the ship goes on and on non-stop through space, without captain, without control. One might almost say: without hope.[15]

Life on the ship—like life itself—is "a long, hard journey" (IV:4).

Occasionally the tenor of the novel suggests that Aldiss is making theological analogies as well. Marapper refers to the spaceship as a world "entirely surrounded by a sort of thin world where the Giants can get and we can't" (IV:1), implying a realm of spiritual life unattainable to mortals. Yet the giants are revealed as merely human—neither gods nor gods' agents. Earlier, Marapper assumes that the ship is controlled by an unseen captain, an inaccessible madman who remains isolated while the crew is "punished for this sin our forefathers committed" (II:2). Yet there is no captain, and the ship is maintained by ignorant humans—there is no deity to provide an orderly world.

Complain and the others have inherited the language of their ancestors, while losing its referents. Words—frequently overtly religious—

degenerate into meaningless sounds. "Jesus knows" becomes "Jeezer's nose"; "for heaven's sake" becomes "for hem's sake"; "Hell" transposes into "hull." Each successive instance blurs the distinctions between words and reality. "God" becomes a "mild swearword" (I: 3) divorced from a sense of divinity. Biblical passages are inverted: "the truth never set anyone free" (I:4). Within the ship, contemporary religious values are meaningless, emphasizing humanity's isolation in time and space.

Nor are religion and politics Aldiss' only targets. The Teachings of the ship equally invert contemporary psychology, based on a trinity of "Froyd, Yung, and Bassit," and define man as "full of ghouls and evil treasures, leeches, and the lusts that burn like acid. . . . a creature of infinite complexity and horror" (II:3). Through inversions, puns, satire, and manipulations of human motives, *Non-Stop* seems clearly an attempt to define Aldiss' own place and time.

Through these structures and themes, Aldiss frames his conclusion, which Gillespie claims is "perhaps the most spectacular . . . of any of Aldiss' novels."[16] Spectacular it is, but also abrupt: Aldiss tries to explain everything, returning from allegory and analogy to science fiction—creating a conclusion that seems rushed, cobbled together.[17] He has, of course, begun preparing early: telepathic moths figure in section II, where he also describes emergency doors that seal off each deck.[18] Yet the disintegration of the ship seems fortuitous, with a cloud of moths suddenly appearing in the machinery of the control room, parodying the traditional *deus ex machina*. Gillespie refers to the scene as "marvelously contrived," meaningful in its relation to Complain while simultaneously "a metaphor for all those who use science to construct new worlds without taking responsibility for what they imagine." Jameson refers to a "twist ending" but argues that such is consistent in a novel which has itself shifted generic protocols to manipulate its readers.[19]

Ultimately, *Non-Stop* is not merely conventional science fiction. It undercuts the genre, shifting the reader's expectations, reaching a conclusion as much accidental as integral; yet that conclusion is consonant with the purposes and themes of the novel and bears a startling resemblance to the final pages of *Helliconia Spring* and *Helliconia Winter*, as if the intervening decades had sharpened Aldiss' narrative powers without altering his underlying vision. It is a serious book, in spite of puns, linguistic inversions, stylistic and structural experimentation, that has an overriding sense of a good story well told.

Notes

[1] The American edition (Criterion, 1959) was re-titled *Starship*, which explicitly reveals the central plot twist.

[2] *Manchester Guardian*, 8 May 1958, p. 8.

[3] *Times Literary Supplement*, 9 May 1958, p. 258.

[4] *New York Herald Tribune*, 20 September 1959, p. 15.

[5] Fredric Jameson, "Generic Discontinuities in SF: Brian W. Aldiss' *Starship*," *Science Fiction Studies*, I, No. 2 (1973), p. 59.

[6] Jameson, p. 63.

[7] *All About Venus* (New York: Dell, 1968), p. 31.

[8] Note especially III:3—the "long journey into darkness"—and IV:5—the physical and mental changes in humans.

[9] Jameson, p. 61.

[10] Jameson, pp. 62-63.

[11] Samuel R. Delany, "Some Reflections on SF Criticism," *Science Fiction Studies*, 25 (November 1981), 233-239; "Generic Protocols: Science Fiction and Mundane," in *The Technological Imagination: Theories and Fictions*, ed. Theresa de Laurentis, Andreas Huyssen and Kathleen Woodward (Madison, WI: Coda, 1980), pp. 175-193.

[12] Jameson, p. 63.

[13] Aldiss, like Piers Anthony, seems to touch on Calhoun's experiments with the effects of overcrowding on rats (see Collings, *Piers Anthony* [Mercer Island, WA: Starmont, 1983], pp. 17, 25). See also Aldiss' short story "Total Environment."

[14] Jameson, p. 58.

[15] For other examples, see III:3; IV:4; III:2; II:1.

[16] Jameson, p. 63.

[17] Similar weak conclusions mar *Bow Down to Nul* (1960; reprinted as *The Interpreter* [1961]).

[18] It fits well into Jameson's analysis that this information appears in the "cognitive" section of the novel.

[19] Jameson, pp. 59-60.

IV

Decade the 1960s:
Vanguard from Alpha, Bow Down to Nul, Hothouse

Aldiss published four short novels prior to *Hothouse*: *Vanguard from Alpha* (1959), *Bow Down to Nul* (1960), *The Primal Urge* (1961), and *The Male Response* (1961). Only the first two are strictly science fiction, and none represents Aldiss' talents well. *Vanguard*, like other science fiction of the period, focuses on "them"—aliens from space who resemble us and who represent the first wave of conquerors.[1] The novel also shows the same concern for explanation that marred *Non-Stop*. *Bow Down to Nul*[2] expands on the alien threat: Earth has been conquered. Humans are aliens on their own world, breathing through special filters in the enclosed cities the Nuls have built. Both novels are full of action and are engaging as the plots unfold. However, each is ultimately flawed; both conclude weakly. *Vanguard* becomes a play on variation—one enemy turns out to be a friend, and the secret of saving the human race an illusion. In *Bow Down to Nul*, the final pages are a rush of explanation, speeding through events with more force than finesse. Still, the final twist is both unusual and Aldissian. Earth is rescued but not through individual, Heinleinian heroics. Instead, the humans succeed by accident. Both novels provide insight into Aldiss' early development but seem more interesting as artifacts than as novels.

Much the same is true of *The Primal Urge* and *The Male Response*. The first includes a science-fictional element—a telltale which, when implanted on an individual's forehead, "pinks" at sexual arousal, thus eliminating the hypocrisy that culture and society foster. Little is made of the device, however, as Aldiss concentrates on the psychology and sociology of human relationships, using the telltale more for its symbolic value. The lurid cover of the paperback edition, in fact, underlines the contradiction between the ostensibly science-fictional theme and the novel's exploitation of sexual possibilities. Aldiss moves between the two with some adroitness. The science-fictional elements set the novel in the near future and suggest unleashed but potential (and potent) sexuality which is in fact rarely realized. By the end, however, the novel seems to have been captured between two conflicting genres.[3]

The Male Response is even less science-fictional. The initial plot involves the purchase of a supercomputer by a developing African nation. Once beyond that point, however, Aldiss again concentrates on psychology. Although an interesting attempt, it does not suggest Aldiss' full powers.

15

In 1962, Aldiss published one of his most impressive and important novels, *Hothouse*.[4] Based on a series of short stories published in *The Magazine of Fantasy and Science Fiction* in 1961, which were awarded the Hugo in 1962, the completed novel represents "great structural skill and a significant advance over his thematically assembled short story collections." Unlike the preceding science-fiction novels, *Hothouse* avoids the sense of a rushed ending. It resists the pressure to explain the scientific supports for the plot. There is, in fact, little of the scientific explanation assumed necessary for science fiction beyond generalized discussions of entropy, causing Mathews to ask in what sense *Hothouse* can even be considered science fiction.[5]

Yet that is precisely the strength of the novel; it rarely seems compelled to explain at all, largely because it cannot truly do so. It describes a series of Odyssean wanderings across a planet that is simultaneously an Earth altered beyond recognition and a psychological map leading from innocence to experience. Aldiss the map-maker enjoys devising exotic species but rarely explains them.[6] His traversers, for example, are spacefaring vegetable-spiders whose webs extend from the Earth to the Moon. Whether such creatures could exist is entirely beyond the point of the novel; that they *do* exist provides for both plot development and clarification of imagery (the ancient Earth is literally covered with spider webs).

Still, *Hothouse* does not break entirely with the earlier novels. It suggests a successful return to the techniques of *Non-Stop* on both a grander and a smaller stage. The landscape has widened from a single ship to include Earth and Moon, expanding Aldiss' possibilities enormously while still retaining the image of characters weaving their way through the overgrown jungles of a spaceship-planet. Gren's world is larger and its movements more cosmic in scope, but his journeys parallel Complain's.

The characters in *Hothouse* continue the physical decline described in *Non-Stop,* although not because of an infusion of alien protein into their systems; they simply devolve in a world surfeited with plant life. Gren and his kind are small, less than a fifth the size of his forebears. They have become, almost literally, the "little green men" of popular science-fictional, alien mythology. And their smallness extends beyond merely physical size. Human culture and civilization have diminished. Language has narrowed, restricting the possibilities of human thought. Lily-yo, a key figure in the opening chapters, "could not express her thoughts. In this green existence there were few thoughts and fewer words. . . . Nor could she herself frame deeper words; human understanding tricked shallow these days" (8)[7]. Aldiss' world makes literal Marvell's poetic vision of

> Far other worlds, and other seas;
> Annihilating all that's made

To a green thought in a green shade.

("The Garden," 46–48)

Language parallels the Earth itself, moving entropically to a semi-comic reduction of names to nursery rhymes. The exotic vegetable-creatures of a million-years hence lack any logical taxonomy consistent with humanity's present aggrandizement of science. Instead, the creatures are called by simplistic, rhyming names: "dripperlip," "burnurn," "whistle-thistle," "wiltmilt," "speedseed," "crocksock," "fuzzypuzzle," and "bellyelm." More sophisticated terminology would surpass the characters' abilities to understand and remember—the rhyming mnemonics suggest the paucity of intellect and imagination in the characters. Other names—particularly "termight," "treebee," and "plantant"—are pointedly puns, altering contemporary words to fit new referents. "Termights," for example, are distant descendants of termites, but in a world in which humans and insects are the same size (or humans are smaller) and insects better equipped to survive, "termights" seems more appropriate.

Aldiss' description of remnant humanity emphasizes their precarious state. They are unaware of complexity within their own lives, existing only to escape multiple predators. Their huts, he writes, consist of hollowed out "homemaker nuts," attached to branches with the "distilled cement from the acteoyle plant" (I:1). Yet this complexity escapes Gren's people. To them, the structures are simply "nuthuts." Aldiss' future Earth is a Swiftian nightmare, in which his Lilliputians literally live in nuts, use thorns for swords, and are the rightful prey of motile vegetable life.

As the novel progresses, the diminutive humans are further reduced. They lose their few possessions and are carried beyond their usual territory, leaving behind their hutnuts. They literally lose their souls, small carved totems that drop unnoticed as two characters "play the sandwich game," i.e., engage in intercourse. By the end of their journeys, they have been stripped of everything we might consider basic to civilization.

Even more critically, a distinctive characteristic of humanity—creative intelligence—has been apportioned to other creatures. Most of Gren's intellectual development results from his symbiotic relationship with the fungoid morel. He provides nourishment: the morel provides intellect, opening Gren's mind to new possibilities. In later chapters, Gren escapes his intellectual subservience to the morel, only to become physically subservient to the piscean Sodal Ye. Unable to move on land, the Sodal uses Gren as a beast of burden, while it alone understands the imminent destruction of the Earth, a stage in the cycles of growth and degeneration, life and death, creation and destruction that form the novel.

All of this is to say that even though Gren is the central character of *Hothouse,* he is not necessarily its hero. Many episodes draw on his perspectives, but just as often, he is ignored as Aldiss follows alternate developments. Or, in the latter chapters, Gren is so entirely subsumed by the morel—physically and psychologically—that Aldiss transfers attention

17

to Gren's mate Yattmur. In addition, Gren is largely incapable of heroic actions in a world of potential death. In the opening pages, he is a petulant man-child, problematical and trouble-bringing. He must be protected by the women of his tribe but only because of an accident of sex; he has the potential to reproduce in a world in which death is omnipresent. He acts impulsively, his actions resulting in the violent deaths of his fellows. And finally, he is exiled by his own, an act tantamount to execution. By the time he has reduced his companions and protector-females to one, Poyly, he has already been taken over by the morel and is no longer acting on his own.

As Gren and Poyly travel, spurred by the morel's obsession with dividing itself and literally taking over the world, Gren becomes more and more alienated from his companion and from the reader. He refuses to remain on a secure island, even though the place provides the only semblance of peaceful existence the humans have ever experienced. Later, wholly under the control of the morel, he plots to destroy his own son by letting the morel infect the child as well. When the morel is removed (not by Gren, but by Yattmur acting under the directions of the Sodal Ye), Gren is forced to carry the Sodal, becoming an animal in function. Only in the final pages, when he must choose between remaining in his doomed jungle-home or leaving with his transformed former companions Lily-yo and Haris, only then does Gren act consciously. He is, as he argues, "tired of carrying or being carried" (Ch. 23). He rejects the traveler metaphor of a continued journey of exploration and elects to remain in the world he has known, where "danger was my cradle, and all we have learned will guard us!" In a passage more Miltonic than science-fictional, Gren and his mate walk hand in hand "down into a bower of leaves," returning to their paradise.

Readers looking for a hero who pits himself against the odds of a hostile environment (as in Harry Harrison's Deathworld novels) will be disappointed. On the hothouse–Earth, humanity is more accident than actor. Souls have become wooden totems (foreshadowing the Phagorian totems of Helliconia); humans pass quickly and ephemerally, particularly in the opening chapters. Aldiss takes pains to create sympathetic characters, such as Poyly, then destroys the characters suddenly and without any apparent regret. Such is merely the way of life on a dying Earth— another thematic and structural connection with Helliconia.

But there are potential "heroes" in *Hothouse*. The banyan tree, for example, has grown through millennia until it controls an entire continent. In a world of death, it survives to spread over its "vegetable empire," another touch of Andrew Marvell. Or perhaps the heroic figure is the fecund Earth itself, moving toward destruction as the sun threatens to nova. In spite of all, it continually engenders life, crowding itself with motile, sentient vegetable forms, evolving new creatures to replace devolving man. The vegetable creatures are as awesome in their powers and ferocity as the humans' names for them are poverty-stricken in imagina-

18

tion and intellectual depth. Or perhaps the true protagonists are entropy, time, and the cycles of life and death, growth and decay, as Aldiss details the slowing of Earth and Moon in their orbits, the massing of vegetable life-essence for its final push into space in an attempt to defeat decay and destruction.

However one resolves the question of a hero, *Hothouse* remains impressive. It is, in its own way, as misdirecting as *Non-Stop,* suggesting a novel on the order of Alan Dean Foster's later *Midworld,* in which adventure would be paramount and conventional science-fictional heroism fully developed. Instead, we examine a Lilliputian humanity,[8] silhouetted against a world more vigorous and powerful than man. Characters are ephemeral, appearing and disappearing with frustrating rapidity. Plot itself seems more an exercise in Odyssean mapmaking than in delineating carefully structured episodes. The conclusion itself is, as we might expect from *Non-Stop,* ambiguous. Gren remains where he began, returning to the hothouse of the forest in spite of new choices available to him. It is a victory, yet one tainted with defeat, since the world itself is about to die.

Hothouse is, in final estimation, intriguing, an artful blend of adventure with statement, action with image, excitement with theme and message. It explores stasis, entropy, change, and meaning, pitting a remnant humanity against a world grown too large, too threatening. *Hothouse* defines through metaphor and image precisely the plight contemporary humanity must face and somehow overcome.

Notes

[1] For a brief discussion of aliens in 1950s science fiction, see Andrew Griffin, "Sympathy for the Werewolf," in *The Borzoi College Reader,* 5th ed, ed. Charles Muscatine and Marlene Griffith (New York: Random House, 1984), 647–48. (Rpt. of original publication, University Publishing [Winter 1979]).

[2] Also published under the title "X for Exploitation" in *New Worlds SF* (March, April, May 1960) and as *The Interpreter* (London: Digit, 1961).

[3] For a discussion of the differences between science fiction, fantasy, and pornography, see Eric S. Rabkin, *The Fantastic in Literature* (Princeton, NJ: Princeton University Press, 1976), 49–50, 73; William Irwin, *The Game of the Impossible: A Rhetoric of Fantasy* (Urbana, IL: University of Illinois Press, 1976), 89–91. Both separate pornography from either science fiction or fantasy.

[4] "Hothouse" (February 1961), "Nomansland" (April 1961), "Undergrowth" (July 1961), "Timberline" (September 1961), and "Evergreen" (December 1961). For a critical analysis of *Hothouse* and a discussion of alterations in the text for the American edition, retitled *Long Afternoon of Earth,* see Joseph Milicia's introduction to *Hothouse* (New York: Baen, 1984), 1–18. Milicia concludes that "Though the vision of life on earth in *Hothouse* is predominantly somber—alternately gruesome, sardonic and elegiac—the sheer cornucopian inventiveness of the novel, from the comic names to cosmic panoramas, is exhilarating, and its very excess gives the tale of exotic life forms and awesome dangers a special kind of unity" (15).

[5] Mathews, *Aldiss Unbound,* p. 18.

19

[6]Gillespie, "Literature Which Awakens Us," p. 166.

[7]Citing *Long Afternoon of Earth* (New York: Signet, 1962), an abridged U.S. reprint of the British *Hothouse* (London: Faber, 1962).

[8]Recently, Casey Fredericks has commented on the Swiftian echoes in Aldiss, countering Wingrove and Griffin's approach to the novels in *Apertures* (*Science-Fiction Studies,* 11 [November 1984], 339–40).

V
Decade the 1960s:
The Dark Light Years, Greybeard, Earthworks

Following *Hothouse,* Aldiss' novels turned toward darkness: *The Dark Light Years* (1964) is a Swiftian "excremental vision" of aliens who live surrounded by their own waste; *Greybeard* (1964) is atmospherically and thematically dark; and *Earthworks* (1965), which begins on a "death ship," concludes (in Colin Greenland's terms) "exhausted and misanthropic."[1] Aldiss' themes are logical outgrowths of earlier explorations into adaptability; incidental characters appear and disappear with disconcerting rapidity, while central characters define moments critical to themselves and to the species as a whole.[2] Complain destroys the ship: Gren returns to the forest. *The Dark Light Years* concludes with an incipient freedom neither wholly realized nor wholly defined. *Greybeard* ends with the discovery of children and suggests the immense difficulties and challenges that discovery entails. *Earthworks* seems the most ambiguous of all: Noland is about to assassinate a political figure and precipitate a nuclear war . . . to *save* humanity. In each instance, the novel ends where other writers might have begun. Characters attain to awarenesses that justify their histories and hold out promises, but Aldiss refuses to define those promises. If he has done his job (and he has), we understand the momentum of the characters through territories unmapped even by Aldiss himself, whose concern lies more with the process of thought and experience leading to knowledge and understanding than with action for its own sake.

The Dark Light Years is an ambiguous novel, rather short yet ranging through space to distant worlds, back to an Earth almost identical to ours, then out again to discover the consequences of human stupidity. Many of Aldiss' fictions suggest a humanity that is almost "majestic," as Greenland argues, but Aldiss is not blind to the alternative: "man as seedy, squalid, and stupid, the spoiler of planets."[3] In *DLY,* man is the destroyer. The narrative begins with an aging human in an enclosure on an alien planet, but the second episode, told from the alien perspective, describes the Utods' arrival on Grudgrodd (Utodian for "mistake") and their subsequent encounter with thin-shaped creatures which land there. Delighted at the prospect of communicating with aliens, the Utods rush forward. In their blindness to anything except terrestrial determinants for intelligence, however, the humans slaughter most of the Utods.

This initial failure to communicate reverberates throughout the novel.

21

The aliens are almost too successfully "other"; the humans understand neither their speech nor their perceptions. Yet since the Utodians have much to teach humanity, Aldiss explores their philosophies, religions, and history. Both Mathews and Greenland discuss Utodian attitudes toward eschatology, nature, and death, suggesting that these lie at the heart of the novel. Neither, however, focuses on an obvious "key" to the narrative, a single signpost that identifies Aldiss' new territory. Greenland comments that Aldiss' "sole crime against [SF] orthodoxy . . . is to bring on the shit . . . ," a comment reminiscent of Ellison's.[4] For all of their exotic philosophy and communication structures, the Utods remain essentially alien in this particular: they worship their own excrement. They are confused when the humans constantly wash away the waste products accumulating about the great creatures in their cage at the Exozoo. The humans see the Utods as hogs wallowing in filth; after all, for the humans, civilization represents "the distance man has placed between himself and his excreta" (Ch. 5).[5]

The narrative, however, argues that humanity has become distanced not only from its excreta but from its world and from itself. "Natural" foods are disparaged by a government "pushing the new poison-free manmade foods and drinks" (Ch. 7); pedestrians wear street masks to isolate them from polluted air; warfare is neither seen nor felt, but abstracted onto a distant planet, Charon.[6] Humanity has in fact attempted to divorce itself from its environment.

The attempt fails, even though the characters do not realize it. Sir Mihaly Pasztor, Director of the Exozoo, may boast of his civilization, but he and his fellows live as much in their cultural excreta as do the Utods: rubbish litters his environment; waste from cars poisons his air (Ch. 7). By ignoring conditions, humanity tries to cut itself off from its own nature. Aldiss does not argue that we should worship excrement, only that we recognize it as part of life. Pasztor finally understands this and makes the first serious move toward communicating with the aliens: "removing his trousers, squatting close to them, speaking gently, the Director of the Exozoo defecated onto the plastic floor" (Ch. 7).

The moment of understanding comes too late, however. Humanity continues to descend into its own particular excrement: warfare, greed, selfishness, separation. The novel concludes at the locale of the first scene—an enclosure on Grudgrodd. Forty years have passed; warfare has destroyed most of Earth as well as a number of other planets, including the Utods' home. The human is rescued by his fellows, leaving the Utods alone on the planet. The final paragraph suggests the open-endedness common in Aldiss' narratives. The Utods watch the departing humans, then the younger one examines the abandoned weaponry in the enclosure:

> Satisfied, he turned back and walked without pause through the gate of the stockade. He had remained patiently captive for a small fraction of his life. Now it was time that he thought about freedom.

Time, too, that the rest of his brothers thought about free-dom. (Ch. 13)

That freedom is precisely what remnant humanity seems destined never to discover.

In spite of the serious theme, *DLY* is not unremittingly serious. Greenland says that "embittered and depressing as his lapsarian image of man may sound, Aldiss' comic method and surprisingly gentle touches are those of a man who accepts humanity, and an author who is not ready to write it off."[7] The novel is insistently humorous. Names, for instance, are both self-conscious and suggestive: the irony of Pasztor, or Ainson ("only" son), or Melmoth with its reflection of Gothic horror. The word *utod* suggests the German *tod*, "death," a reasonable suggestion in light of the concentration on death in the novel. The Utodian language is almost comic in its clumsiness: words such as *Dapdrof* or *Grudgrodd* remind us of Broddingnag and serve much the same purpose as Swift's language. *DLY* may indict humanity as a species, but it does so with tenderness and humor, although Griffin and Wingrove argue that this leads to the novel's most serious failure:

> Throughout, it wavers between the need to entertain the SF reader and a desire to reveal Man's essential dark nature. Its mood is inconsistent and its occasional whimsicality suggests a real lack of feeling. At times it seems as if Aldiss was afraid to touch his subject matter raw. . . . He errs on the side of caution . . . and distances himself behind an often flippant irony.[8]

In spite of such difficulties, however, *DLY* both entertains and instructs, holding true to Aldiss' purposes.

Greybeard is less overtly humorous and dogmatic, but more success-ful. Gillespie parallels it with *Hothouse*, the tones in each being typically Aldiss: "a mixture of vibrant ebullience, English jollity, pungent irony, and acute melancholia which tells of people who find joy in living al-though they 'have lost all the world.' "[9] Indeed, in *Greybeard*, we have lost the future. The novel is appropriately dark. Willis McNelly refers to it as "muted, sad, pessimistic, autumnal"; the world, he says, "has begun to end, not with a bang, but with a whimper, and Aldiss tells the story of that whimper."[10]

The novel links with Aldiss' earlier works: Griffin and Wingrove see it, for example, as providing the "synthesis of the thesis of *Non-Stop* and the antithesis of *Hothouse*."[11] Unlike those novels, however, *Greybeard* does not seem an adolescent piece; it is not concerned with growth and maturity. It emphasizes age burdened by self-imposed barrenness. Algy Timberlane, "Greybeard," is in his fifties, one of the youngest people left on Earth. But like Gren under the influence of the morel, he refuses to sit and stagnate. Instead, he wanders through his world, mapping its contours as he comes to understand them. The world he finds is increas-ingly static and senescent, but Greybeard insists upon exploring it.

Structurally, *Greybeard* also parallels the earlier novels. It is an Odyssey, with the river as both literal roadway and image of flux in an increasingly static world. Like the ship in *Non-Stop* or the traversers in *Hothouse,* the river transforms Greybeard's reminiscences into something at once elegiac and nostalgic, as the narrative shifts from a hopeless future back to the beginnings of the catastrophe, each time further back, until we see Greybeard's childhood as Algy Timberlane, one of the last surviving children born on Earth. Chapters 1, 3, 5, and 7 describe England between 2029 and 2032, while Chapter 2 looks backward to 2018, Chapter 4 to 2000, and Chapter 6 to 1982. By fracturing conventional time-flow, Aldiss moves from an elegiac, poetic texture to a more objective tone and back again—while simultaneously suggesting directions he will later explore in *An Age* and *Frankenstein Unbound.* Over all presides the figure of the grey wanderer: "Death stood impatiently over the land, waiting to count his last few pilgrims" (ch. 1).

The novel begins in decay and death, contrasting with the lushness of *Hothouse.* Within a world "told in tones of grey," Aldiss concentrates on entropy and devolution. There is, Greybeard tells himself, only "a road leading downhill" (Ch. 2). In *Hothouse,* vegetable life had replaced mammalian. In *Greybeard,* dogs, cats, and cattle are replaced by their wild cousins, the reindeer and the fox. Civilized humanity is likewise replaced as Aldiss explores transformed living patterns and relationships, with humans described as resembling wolves, apes, or the living tree bark (Ch. 1). Later, he compares humans simply with graves (Ch. 3). In the earlier novels, landscapes became increasingly "human"; here humanity merges with the earth itself.

Building incrementally on this sense of human devotion, Aldiss alludes to Shakespeare's Seven Ages of Man, of which only the last remains. The stagnation of individuals mirrors the stagnation of society as a whole. Likewise, just as Timberlane had become an old man, almost indistinguishable from the wilderness itself, so human knowledge and science have become superstition; vitamin pills strung like magic beads act as a talisman promising immortality. And the memory of children fades into a rumor of gnome-like creatures wandering the forest.

In such a world, Aldiss suggests, Earth's ecology might be improved by removing man entirely. Humanity passes: Earth abides. In an apocalyptic passage in the final chapter, Aldiss portrays an Earth swarming with life, a "great tide of petals, leaves, fur, scales, and feathers. Nothing could stem it . . ." (Ch. 7). Mankind, it seems, was but a temporary aberration, a momentary phenomenon disturbing the development of life on Earth. Without human interference, one character decides, the land had "never looked better," foreshadowing Aldiss' dissection of human interference in *Earthworks.*

Yet *Greybeard* is more than a paean to ecology. Its central issue is not the relationship between human and the environment, but between human and human. Because of "The Accident," as a nuclear disaster is euphemistically called, there are no more children. Humanity is dying of attrition from a sterility directly linked to man's tampering with the environment. Aldiss explicitly refers to that tampering in terms of sexuality and sterility. The adults of the 1960s, he writes,

> ... were like savages who had to go through some fearful initiation rite. Yes, that was it, an initiation rite, and if they had come through it, then perhaps they might have grown up into brave and wise adults. But the ceremony had gone wrong. Too frenzied by far, it had not stopped short at circumcision: the whole organ had been lopped off. (Ch. 2)

Timberlane joins a group of scientists dedicated to recording the history of the Accident and its aftermath. With biting irony, however, Aldiss names the group the "Documentation of Universal Contemporary History" (Europe), creating the acronym "douche"—uniquely appropriate for an organization studying humanity's sterility.

Through flashback, the reader understands more about the nature of the catastrophe. Not only did nuclear explosions in space sterilize all higher mammals on Earth, but the surviving children were destroyed by adults fighting for possession of them (Ch. 4), until finally, confronted by the spectre of a childless future, the human race virtually gives up, like the childless adults of Clarke's *Childhood's End*.

The underlying villain of the novel is less humanity in the abstract than the values of twentieth-century Western society, a point to which Aldiss returns continually, culminating in his creation of Helliconia. Gillespie notes that the final flashback recalls a world of "television pundits . . . 'euphoric about world conditions.' It is our world in all but fine details."[12] Aldiss' theme throughout the novel is that twentieth-century societal values are inimical to continued life; to that end both the straight-line time sequences in the River chapters and the flashbacks in alternating chapters describe a society which destroys children—overtly, through the physical destruction of the Accident, and covertly, through sociological and psychological pressures defined by Timberlake's parents and their relationships.

The theme is further developed in the climactic scene of the novel, in which, after spending over two-hundred pages mourning the loss of children, Greybeard shoots the first child he discovers. An exploiter and fraud named Bunny Jingadangelow strikes to the core of the issue when he says that "the biggest menace any child could face would be—human society!" (Ch. 7). This child is not killed; there is at least that degree of optimism in Aldiss' vision. Greybeard dresses the wound, and the novel concludes with Greybeard and company setting off again down the river, the child stretched out beside them. "They can be taught not to fear us," Greybeard asserts, while his wife Martha reminds him that these children are "virtually a new race." There is a mixture of loss and hope in the final paragraphs, epitomized by the child's new name, Arthur—Timberlane's father's name, and thus a link between past and future. It also suggests the Arthur of Old Britain, a figure promising return and regeneration. Contemporary humanity has almost destroyed the world and has been succeeded by the "gnomes," creatures more closely wedded to the Earth than they. In spite of the optimistic touches, the novel ends ambiguously. The river voyage, with its Homeric, Odyssean overtones, is incomplete. The immensely difficult task of locating the children and teaching them to trust the older generation has not yet even begun. The future is clouded; Greybeard "turned his head, resting one hand on his rifle while with the other he shaded his brow and pretended to gaze ahead at the horizon where the hills were" (Ch. 7). Hope comingles with unease; we find pretense rather than reality, hills shrouded by distance rather than scenes of arrival. As with Complain, Gren, Towler (of *Bow Down to Nul*), and the Utods, Greybeard has arrived at the beginning of a larger journey, one for which his current journey has only begun to prepare him.

Although *Greybeard* is one of Aldiss' most satisfying novels, it does have several flaws. The first is Greybeard himself, a "mature character . . . who reacts to the world rather as Aldiss would like to," as Gillespie says.[13] He is strong and admirable but becomes so introspective that he at times becomes merely a mouthpiece, losing his independence as character. In addition, because Aldiss' characters are strongly delineated, mature, self-willed, and active, it is often difficult to see them as octogenarians. Even Aldiss' suggestion that from children adults grow and from adults children grow again seems incomplete.

These fairly minor points aside, however, the novel remains strong, developing its theme while remaining interesting and engaging. Aldiss blends action and contemplation, description and narration. His interweaving of time is perhaps one of the novel's most successful explorations and is supported in the text by frequent references to the subjectivity of time, an issue Aldiss would take up again in *An Age*.[14] On the whole, *Greybeard* stands as one of Aldiss' signal achievements.

The third novel in this triad, *Earthworks*, is short, compressed, almost dessicated.[15] The narrator-hero, Knowle Noland (whose name suggests the novel's primary theme), is less stable than Greybeard, existing in a world less stable than Greybeard's. Overpopulation and overconsumption have sterilized the soil; air is unbreathable; life in the cities crowded and dangerous; and life in the country a virtual death-sentence, a punishment for minor infractions. The novel begins with a death-ship and ends with the threat of global war as the only remaining solution. Between, we find episodes equally stark and depressing. Noland is divorced from the land, as are his contemporaries. He is out of place in a world of automated freighters, of farms where it is fatal to breathe the air, of intrigue devoted to destroying a destructive stability. The book, as Aldiss indicated in a letter to Larry Ashmead, speaks to those in the " 'Rachel Carson belt,' worried by the use of pesticides, too much artificial fertilizer, etc., on the land."[16]

Earthworks seems at once a culmination and a transition, completing the triad of dark works begun in *DLY* and carrying to logical extremes the ecological collapse Aldiss hinted at there and defined by negation in *Greybeard*. And it, too, concludes ambiguously. Noland moves toward a window slit and an assassination that will change society and might restore the Earth. That restoration, however, is not defined in the novel. Instead Aldiss carries us to the moment of decision and then leaves us, along with his hero, to develop the consequences of that action. He fills in the map, but only partially; for the rest, we must turn to ourselves.

Notes

[1] Colin Greenland, *The Entropy Exhibition*, p. 70.

[2] Greenland, p. 75.

[3] Greenland, p. 84.

[4] Greenland, p. 77; Ellison, *Dangerous Visions*, p. 155.

[5] Excretion, as both natural and intrinsically an act of worship suggests Stapledon's *Sirius*; see my "Of Lions and Lamp-Posts: C. S. Lewis' *The Lion, The Witch, and The Wardrobe* as Response to Olaf Stapledon's *Sirius*," *Christianity & Literature* (Fall 1983), pp. 33–38.

[6] Aldiss' use of Charon foreshadows the Helliconia novels, in which Charon plays an equally important (if largely offstage) part as the entrance to an imagistic Hell—the Earth.

[7] Greenland, *Entropy*, 76–77; see also Griffin and Wingrove, *Apertures*, p. 75.

[8] Griffin and Wingrove, p. 77.

[9] Gillespie, "Literature Which Awakens Us," p. 169; see Griffin and Wingrove, pp. 93–94 for their discussion of connections between *Greybeard, Hothouse,* and *Non-Stop.*

[10] Willis McNelly, "Brian W. Aldiss," in *Science Fiction Writers,* ed. E. F. Bleiler (New York: Scribners, 1982), p. 256.

[11] Griffin and Wingrove, p. 86.

[12] Gillespie, p. 171.

[13] Gillespie, p. 175.

[14] Alterations in time have played at least minor roles in every Aldiss novel since his first. In *Greybeard,* characters openly speculate about the nature of time and space and their relation to human existence. Aldiss retreats somewhat in the misanthropic *Earthworks* (although even there he avoids straight-line narration, using the narrative time-distortion of *Greybeard*), but again returns to this problem with full attention in *An Age, Barefoot in the Head,* and *Report on Probability A,* in which time virtually ceases. In later works, particularly *The Malacia Tapestry* and the Helliconia volumes, time-distortion is again a frequent motif.

[15] A "Doubleday Publicity Questionnaire" dated 20 July 1965, gives the following summary of *Earthworks*:

Knowle Noland may be taken as a typical representative of the future world of EARTHWORKS. Sold by his parents when a child to a strange old junk-collector called March Jordill, he escapes into the teeming platform cities when Jordill is arrested by the police. Later, Noland is himself arrested, and made to work on the land—a stiff punishment at this time, for under all the chemical dosages the exhausted soil receives, the face of the earth is about as hospitable as the surface of Mars.

Eventually, Noland escapes from his penal servitude and joins the Travellers, who are almost the only free men left. Recaptured, he is saved by an unexpected turn of fate and eventually consigned a job on one of the great semi-automatic freighters that ply the oceans of the world. The "Trieste Star" carries sand from Africa's Skeleton Coast to be turned into soil elsewhere. Noland wrecks the ship, and after a number of hazardous adventures in an exotic new African city, comes once more to face the man who is either his greatest friend or his greatest enemy.

The story is told by Noland, section by section. In counterpoint to his own adventures goes another story: one of political conspiracy, as a powerful group—among which is the tantalizing and complex Justine Smith, with whom Noland falls dangerously in love—plots to start a global war.

The way in which Noland's character is worn down, the way he operates almost without thought in the hazardous conditions of his times, the sickness of the soul which dogs him, is vividly depicted until, in the final scenes, Noland must decide what he is, what he hopes for, and what desperate course of action is necessary for the redemption of his tortured world.

Although the mood of the book is grim, there are relief passages of bizarre humor in the usual Aldiss manner. (Huntington Library, San Marino, CA)

[16] "Doubleday Publicity Questionnaire," 20 July 1965. Huntington Library, San Marino, CA.

VI

Decade the 1960s:
An Age, Report on Probability A, and *Barefoot in the Head*

Aldiss' final novels of the 1960s similarly form a triad: *An Age* looks backward stylistically to more conventional novels while exploring Aldiss' interest in the subjectivity of time and distortion of sense perception through drugs, two themes that emerge even more strongly in *Report on Probability A* and *Barefoot in the Head.*

An Age shares much with his earlier novels. It has an ambiguous hero; Edward Bush is not a typical science-fiction adventurer, heroic and impervious. Instead, he is a bit of a coward, at times cruel and self-absorbed. In short, he is a normal human being with the unusual ability to mind-travel through time. The novel also concludes much as we have come to expect with Aldiss—ambiguously—although the final chapter is unusually unsettling. It resolves few major conflicts, instead simply breaking off to force the reader to conclude the text. In Book II, Bush describes a Victorian statue of an Amazon mounted on a stallion, about to "plunge her lance into a tigress which, prompted by reasons of its own, was climbing up and over the horse's shoulder" (Ch. 2). The statue becomes a springboard for a discussion of the Victorians' "what-would-happen-next" art, precisely the sort of art Aldiss creates in the novel. In terms of protagonist and movement, then, *An Age* might be considered "typically" Aldiss.

The novel diverges from earlier pathways, however. Stylistically, it avoids the extremes later explored in *Report* and *Barefoot,* yet it suggests a greater variety of expression than the preceeding three novels, approaching on occasion the lyricism of *Hothouse.* Bush's visions while mind-traveling or Silverstone's explication of startling theories of time attain an almost breathless vividness, while the final chapter plunges the reader from a figurative mountain of revelation into a pedestrian world stultifying in its obsession with the normal.

What truly separates this novel from earlier ones, however, is its expansion of the theme of subjectivity. Aldiss frequently approaches the inwardness of human perception. *Non-Stop,* for example, juxtaposes Complain's assumptions about his world with an external view, emphasizing the differences between them. *Hothouse* juxtaposes Gren's self-awareness with our conception of humanity and human destiny. *Greybeard* introduces the possibility that time itself may be a matter of subjective perception; *An Age* develops that thesis fully.

Although the novel initially seems allied to conventional time-travel narratives, Aldiss adroitly transforms time-travel into something eerier, less stereotypic, more open to possibility. The fundamental mechanism for time-travel becomes the mind; since the body cannot penetrate the surrounding entropy barrier, Aldiss avoids paradox—the travelers cannot alter the past. Instead, they are static observers, cut off from the worlds they enter, invisible to the observed and unable to contact them. Edward Bush has remained in this isolation for two years, abrogating his responsibility to the Wenlock Institute by not returning and his responsibility as an artist by not creating. He is an explorer content to sit on Jurassic sands and watch lobefish evolve.

Gradually, however, Aldiss alters our perceptions, as he has done in earlier novels. Bush returns to an England transformed by ruinously expensive mind-travel into a totalitarian state ruled by General Peregrine Bolt. For a few chapters, Aldiss flirts with an allied sub-genre, the disaster novel, reminiscent of *Earthworks, Greybeard,* and *DLY.* But he ultimately leaves the disaster and its resolution to concentrate on its effects on the unstable character of Edward Bush. Bush is drafted by the regime, systematically degraded and made brutal, and trained to assassinate Silverstone, a time-theoretician hiding in the past. At the end of Book One, Bush resumes mind-traveling, ostensibly to destroy Silverstone.

Book Two again shifts directions. After a brief, tragic interlude in England of the 1930s, Bush "minds" to 1851, meets Silverstone, and joins a revolution within a revolution. Accompanied by a few companions, he "minds" so far into the Cryptozoic that the elements necessary for human respiration have not yet separated out of molten rock. Here Silverstone reveals his full theory of time—that humans have read time backwards. The party has not reached the beginning of time, but its end.

At this point, the writing becomes so fervid that the reader almost believes Silverstone—or is at least willing to contemplate the possibility. Instead of beginning in innocence and moving through experience to sorrow and finally death (frequently an agonizing death, as Bush had discovered in the 1930s episode), humanity is born in suffering and agony and progresses to innocence. The "undermind" within each individual knows the truth, but in the near past (that is, the near future from the reader's perspective) an "overmind" developed, a mental aberration stemming from the discovery that the end of the Earth (its beginning, according to conventional time-frames) was, in geological terms, imminent. From its beginnings "long past, immeasurably long past" as God, humanity had devolved into simpler and simpler states, until it approaches its end in "fire and ash."[1] Understanding this, the "overmind" took control, sparing humanity the "memory" of its ultimate "future" (Book Two; Ch. 8).

The perspective is startling, yet Aldiss has carefully prepared for it. Throughout the novel, Bush dwells on his past and links it to present and future, "as if he symbolically lived his life backwards, muddled in spirit from start to finish" (Book Two; Ch. 1). If Aldiss inverted mores and cultural values in earlier novels, he here suggests an ultimate inversion; as Silverstone puts it, "Every natural law is reversed or shattered" (Book Two; Ch. 7).

The inversion of time parallels the narrative structures Aldiss developed in *Greybeard* and *Earthworks*, where straight-line chronology alternated with flashbacks. Here, however, the manipulation of time has become simultaneously more complex and more simplified. The narrative progresses uninterruptedly from Bush's sojourn in the Jurrassic to his imprisonment in a mental ward. As we move through the narrative, however, we discover that Bush—and everyone else—has been in error, that time moves in the opposite direction and that, as Bush moves forward in subjective time, he is in fact invading his own past. And not incidentally, the readers discover that they are reading a historical novel from their true past (i.e., their apparent future) instead of a speculative novel set in 2093. Time works both ways—and at the end of the novel, Bush (along with the reader) is situated uncomfortably between the two directions.

The relationship between life and art is also central to *An Age*. Bush is an artist, as is his fellow traveler, Borrow. Both are of the vanguard; their function, as Silverstone sees it, is to express the new truths about time through art, to integrate human perception with external reality through art. *An Age* itself is structured to do precisely that.

The discussion of Victorian statuary is one instance of Aldiss' attitude toward art as premonitory rather than complete. The Victorians, Bush argues, were masters at freezing one second into a question, while contemporary art, influenced by photography, cinema, television, and "lasoids," insists upon resolutions (Book Two; Ch. 2). Aldiss' interest lies in the questions, however, in the frozen moment rich with potential.[2] In terms of the novel, the frozen moment possible in art is the closest one can approach the true nature of time, and more than anyone, the artist can approximate it. Aldiss does not mention Holman Hunt, that artist-figure so pervasive in his fictions; here, he refers to Degas and Picasso and then moves on to novelists. But the suggestion made here is precisely the one developed in intricate detail in *RPA*. And even more to the point is Silverstone's discussion of the greatest novelists of his age, Marston Orston, whose *Fullbright*, like Aldiss' *RPA*, concentrates on a static moment. *Fullbright* is a "deliberately unfinished novel, over four million words long, which describes a girl getting up to open her bedroom window" (Book Two; Ch. 6). If, as Silverstone argues, time is bi-dimensional, then the same instant can exist eternally. Approached from the past and from the future, it will repeat itself perpetually. The crux in *An Age* is simply that humanity has not yet discovered this point. We have, in Silverstone's words, "observed wrong, and we did not know what we were doing" (Book Two; Ch. 7), an effective introduction to subjectivity, objectivity, and observation in *RPA*, *Barefoot*, *Malacia*, and Helliconia.

At the same time, however, *An Age* is a strongly realized novel in its own right. It begins rather slowly, deferring its final direction as long as

31

possible, forcing the reader to alter expectations as it shifts from time to time and form to form. But that is what Aldiss has always demanded from his readers. *An Age* is a difficult book, partially because of the manipulation of time and partially because of Aldiss' stylistic devices. Its language is complex and "multi-valued," to borrow a term from *RPA*, emphasizing puns to establish meanings and importance.[3] Aldiss himself has suggested that the novel did not meet his full expectations; "This is my most ambitious novel," he wrote to Ashmead, "and I just did not succeed as well as I had hoped."[4] But Griffin's estimation seems ultimately more valid:

> Whatever one says about the lasting value of *An Age*, there can be no doubt that it is a virtuoso piece of Sf which makes a thrilling read as it draws towards its suitably fantastic climax. If Aldiss had stopped at this point, he would still have earned an accolade for the way in which he combined the traditional virtues of Sf adventure with deeper issues. . . .[5]

Given a chance, the novel repays the reader with an exhilaration and sense of wide-ranging possibility that is a hallmark of science fiction as a genre and Aldiss as a writer.

Aldiss' explorations of time lead neatly into his next published novel, *Report on Probability A*. His discussion of Victorian art in *An Age*, his vision of art as capturing a static moment, leaving the future undefined and asking in effect "what comes next"—all are inherent in *RPA*, in which almost literally nothing happens. Yet to claim that the earlier novel prepared the way for *RPA* is misleading since *RPA* was completed in manuscript by 1962 but rejected when Aldiss approached his publishers. Only after its serialization in *New Worlds* did Faber finally accept it.[6]

As a result, much in *An Age* and *Earthworks* connects them with *RPA*, although *RPA* is a radically different kind of book. Mathews discusses its genesis in the influences of Michel Butor and Alain Robbe-Grillet and the French anti-novel, citing Aldiss' avowed intention to discard many literary conventions and to concentrate on a "lean, hard-surfaced" style.[7] The result was *RPA*, and after its rejection, the artist-as-hero focus of *An Age*.

RPA is ultimately a difficult book, but it nonetheless remains a major achievement. Greenland refers to it as a classic of "the new fiction" of the 1960s. Aldiss' earlier allegiance, he argues, had been to science fiction as the "literature of causality. Man's departures and disasters could be attributed to certain sins of omission and commission," leading to novels in which everything is explained in the final pages, as in *Non-Stop* and *Bow Down to Nul*. In *RPA*, Aldiss rejects this convention and quite simply explains nothing: things, he argues, must "remain unresolved if they are to stand in any way as an equation of life." If the catastrophe of *Greybeard* is placed in the past and revealed gradually and tangentially through interlacing chapters, the sense of human involvement in a catastrophe is nearly missing in *RPA*. The novel "presents no conclusions, only data. Life—and the disaster which has stopped it—is always elsewhere."[8]

Instead, Aldiss forces the reader to interpret raw, undigested data without providing a matrix for interpretation. In addition to the first level of observers—G, S, and C and their obsession with Mr. And Mrs. Mary's house—Aldiss includes multiple levels of observers-being-observed: Domoladossa and Midlakemela, who label the world of G, S, C, and the Marys "Probability A," an alternate frame to their own; the Distinguishers, who watch Domoladossa through the frame around his wife's picture: Congressman Sadlier and Joe Growleths, who observe the Distinguishers through a robot fly intruded into their probability; The Suppressor of the Archives, the Impaler of Distortions, and others watching Joe and his fellows[9]; and others watching them. Over them all, of course, stands Brian Aldiss, watching observers watching observers, and beyond him, the reader. As Joe puts it, one world watches another, in which the inhabitants are studying reports from yet other probabilities; ironically, Joe is unaware of the ranks of observers concentrating on him.

Unfortunately, none of the observers (except Aldiss and the reader) understands what is seen. Domoladossa suggests that the aliens he watches may have "human responses" (Part One, Ch. 3), but he must continue observing them to determine that. His observations, however, undermine that sense of purpose since he consciously avoids identifying particularly human responses. He can note in *his* report that Mrs. Mary was singing but cannot interpolate from that action and assert that she was happy (Part One, Ch. 5). Domoladossa is sure of his own humanity, but the Distinguishers watching him are not. Although they agree that he looks like them, that his world is of "almost co-determinate synchronicity," they have no matrix for defining his scale. He might, according to one observer, "be no bigger than my thumb. He may be as tall as a house" (Part One, Ch. 6). The same problem recurs on each level; there is no *key*, a word repeated throughout the text. Instead, observers must restrict themselves to merely recording data. As the Congressman says, "All we are after is facts. We don't have to decide what reality is, thank God!" (Part Two, Ch. 4).

The difficulty with this is that Aldiss seems intent upon forcing his readers to draw conclusions, even though they also have "no key to scale." Throughout the text, Aldiss focuses on a painting by Holman Hunt, "The Hireling Shepherd." C, S, and G all have copies of it; Hunt is a recognized painter in several of the alternative probabilities, and most telling of all, Aldiss concludes the novel by moving into the painting itself, concentrating on this frozen moment. The novel ends in stasis, in a world of unexplained phenomena and unseen futures: the shepherd leans toward a girl, his flock forgotten, a moth imprisoned in his hand, her hand raised in indecision. "She waited," Aldiss writes, giving the brief statement the full weight of a paragraph, then a final two-word paragraph: "He waited" (Part Three, Ch. 4). Ultimately, nothing happens, no explanations are presented; yet the reader has participated in a dizzying journey through multiple alternative worlds, including his own, becoming in turn observer and observed, a technique Aldiss will return to in the complex layerings of observers in Helliconia.

One of the most frequent critical remarks about Aldiss is that he never writes the same book twice. Even the individual volumes in Helliconia, while clearly a single artistic entity, differ in texture and style. His concerns grow and change, and his novels reflect those changes; in none of his works is style wedded so completely to content as in his two most difficult novels, *RPA* and *Barefoot in the Head*. In *RPA*, Aldiss parallels stylistically objectivity and lack of interpretative keys so completely, focuses so narrowly on the surface details of the map, that we lose sight of how this tiny portion relates to a whole. And this loss is precisely what Aldiss intends.

The opening paragraphs enforce an objectivity at once alien and uncomfortable. Mathews has remarked that the opening sentences are notably negative. They attempt "the most minimal statements, saying what things *are not* rather than what they are: there is no frost, no wind, no rain, no sun, no shadows." [10] The descriptions are inordinately detailed, particularly of G's clock, of some relevance in light of Aldiss' preoccupation with time in *Non-Stop, Greybeard*, and *An Age*. It is, however, even more important to note the syntactic structures Aldiss uses in the opening paragraphs—and throughout the novel.

Where earlier novels began with action, *RPA* consciously avoids it. Although the first two statements of the text contain active verbs—"begins" and "showed"—the sentences carefully limit any sense of overt action. From that point on, verbs are static rather than active. Aldiss relies heavily on "be," "have," and "do" (which some grammarians refer to as a "pro-verb" that stands for an action without specifying it, something like a "pronoun"). Many of the other verbs describe states of being: "remained" or "stood." Of the handful of verbs defining specific, forceful actions, most are coupled with modals and auxiliaries to defuse their sense of action, or negated with the adverbial "not." In either instance, the verbs reinforce the passivity so characteristic of *RPA*. [11]

Aldiss seems intent upon avoiding active verbs, writing sentences that occasionally verge on awkwardness and that could have been more fluid if expressed actively. Aldiss concludes his description of the sun shining into G's bungalow, for example, with "G was never on the couch when the sun was" (Part One, Ch. 1). The final "was" seems ambiguous, yet it suggests the state-of-being that the book explores.

Throughout, Aldiss concentrates on copular verbs that identify rather than define and interpret. A mat "was stretched over the floorboards"—an objective observation as close to approximating reality as the novel allows. Aldiss could have written that the mat "stretched over the floorboards," a minor change at most. Doing so, however, would attribute

34

action—if not volition—to the thing in question, and, as Brian Griffin says, in *RPA,*

> ... while the *things* remain, their life and meaning have largely departed with their true owners. Their life and meaning are not even implied ... by the absence of humanity. Aldiss' anti-novel (his own description of it) is concerned, rather, with the search for those missing ingredients of life and meaning through the mediation of a series of Observers, each of whom may or may not be human, or potentially human.[12]

To endow the mat with volition, even metaphorically, would create a contradiction, since Aldiss is concerned with facts, not with interpretations. His grammatical structures emphasize this interest, leading to a particular (and often peculiar) texture in the novel. *RPA* seems inordinately passive, sedentary, which the avid science-fiction reader might neither understand nor tolerate. Only when Aldiss includes italicized discussions of observers observing observers does the novel approach conventional science fiction. Even there, Aldiss manipulates the reader away from solid, interpretative, assumptive fiction by presenting an infinite present described in obsessive detail, using words which themselves deny any sense of action.

The novel's conclusion underlines Aldiss' strategies, as he shifts from static observers to the Hunt painting, refusing even at the end to interpret. Throughout *RPA,* characters have seen the painting as a key to understanding situations. One character creates an entire fiction around the actions and motives of the painted figures. But finally, Aldiss invalidates even that suggestion of causality and explanation. The novel concludes as it began—in stasis: "She waited. He waited." Aldiss forces the reader back to one of the introductory epigrams, Geothe's "Do not, I beg you, look for anything behind phenomena. They are themselves their own lesson."

If *RPA* is a classic statement on objectivity and the difficulty of interpretation, *Barefoot in the Head* is equally a classic of subjectivity and multi-valued data, defining a world in which nothing is unambiguously itself. Like earlier novels, *Barefoot* stems from a cataclysm, but here the disaster is explained: the Acid Head War, so named because Kuwait dropped hallucinogenic bombs on Europe and America. The people affected are literally "bombed"—stoned. Even those who avoid the most devastating strikes become infected as the pollution spreads. Colin Charteris, the protagonist, is initially only mildly infected. However, as he travels through drug-saturated France and England, his observations, his utterances, and the novel itself become webs of hallucination and distorted perceptions. The novel becomes what Aldiss calls a study in "the ruptures in perceptions of our time."[13] The prose alters until the novel approaches a Joycean complexity; Anthony Burgess' definition of style in Joyce's *Ulysses* as "an endless commentary from the main characters on the data thrown at them by life . . . , sometimes chaotic, following subterranean laws of association rather than logic"[14] seems equally appropriate to *Barefoot*.

Aldiss' altering style—his concern with how language may be interpreted—creates the novel, far more than does plot. There is indeed less a single plot than a series of possibilities dependent upon how one interprets words used to define them.[15] This stylistic emphasis begins early. The first sentence is impersonal and distant, semi-passive: "The city was open to the nomad." But Aldiss quickly plunges into a riot of action: Charteris climbs and stands; machines creak and snap; metals cool. Sentences act as signposts for maps to come: "Sinews and bones flexed and dainty." The syntax here is ambiguous. On a first reading, "flexed" seems verbal, although how bones might flex remains a problem and an apparent mixed metaphor. Upon reaching "dainty," however, the reader must shuffle mental sets and re-define words, with "flexed" most likely functioning as an adjective—and the sentence suddenly has no verb.

This new style denies the precision and objectivity of *RPA*, substituting instead a staggering abundance of possibilities. As the Waiting Man tells Charteris, "The times themselves, I mean, talk nonsense—but the sort of nonsense that makes us simultaneously very skeptical about the old rules of sanity" (Book I, "The Serpent of Kundalini"). Insanity is the rule, as traditional semantic patterns are first disregarded and finally discarded. Charteris must make sense of a "godamnbiguity" of perception and experience that leads him to contemplate such poems as "On the Spontaneous Generation of Ideas During Conversation. Spontagions Ideal Convertagion. The Conflation of Spongation in Idations. Agenbite of Auschwitz" (Book I, "Multi-Value Motorway").[16] Free-association spirals increase, until paragraphs become conflations of puns, exercises in multiplicity. The text mirrors the psychic disintegration of humanity (Charteris repeatedly insists that there has been a "dislocation") until we arrive at such statements as:

> So as the Pleonastocene Age curtled to a closure the banshee crumbled under the chundering gearbox to grow up into deeply scarlet peony by the sacred roadslide where they finely went on foot with Anjie meandering through the twilicker her golden grey goose beside her it in its beak holding gently to her smallest twigged finger with Charteris choked in his throat's silence (Book III, "Ouspenski's Astrabahn").

Along the way, Aldiss pauses to enjoy puns, verbal play, and occasional references to the fictions of A. E. van Vogt, Robert A. Heinlein, and Thomas Disch.

Even while reversing the stylistic directions of *RPA*, however, *Barefoot* consciously builds upon it, as if the two in tandem resolve problems of human perspective from alternate directions. Colin Greenland writes that in *RPA*, Aldiss

. . . shrinks life to the scanty dimensions of the page, eschewing the artificial flavour and colour that fiction normally adds. In *Barefoot* he expands and inflates the page, superimposing text on text, to approach the true multiplicity of life. He will not pretend that the pause between the two can be anything but uncomfortable.[17]

Throughout *Barefoot*, Aldiss echoes *RPA*: "on a calendar, a picture of two people tarrying in a field," their faces fixed in "frozen gestures" (Book I, "The Serpent of Kundalini"); the cry, "Tell us facts" (Book I, "The Serpent of Kundalini"), reminiscent of Congressman Sadlier's simplistic approach to complexity; characters reduced to one-letter initial-names; Kroninkrijk's wife's staring into cameras, memorizing insignificant and unmoving data; and finally, a quotation from *RPA*—"At the same time a dead leaf whisked through the circle of vision over the step and was gone into the darkness that always surrounded the circle of vision." This time, however, there is an addendum: "But none of the watchers any longer cared for the old movements" (Book III, "Ouspenski's Astrabahn").

The world of *Barefoot* incorporates infinite possibilities. One need not interpret data since any interpretation is equally possible and all equally false. If in *RPA* we understand nothing because we do not know the nature of events, in *Barefoot,* we understand nothing because everything is "simultaneously visible from all sides."[18]

Perhaps the best example of this multiplicity is Colin Charteris himself. His name suggests map-making—charting. Taken as a new messiah in Europe, he is referred to as a "saint"; the original Charteris, he tells us, was the English writer who created "The Saint" novels. Yet not even that datum is ultimately helpful since *Charteris* is not even his name. He has, like Melville's Ishmael, merely appropriated it: "That's what I call myself." He is a Serbian, what Angelina later calls a "subservient Dalmatian." So within Charteris himself, we find layerings of meaning, all intentional and most ambiguous.

Much more could be said about *Barefoot in the Head* and has been said by Mathews, Greenland, Griffin and Wingrove, and others.[19] It is complex and difficult, taxing the reader to the utmost and pressing beyond the boundaries of science fiction, conflating science-fictional content and Joycean, mainstream stylistics. "If *Barefoot in the Head* isn't Sf." Greenland concludes, "it is because it is too wide in scope." Griffin notes that while it "may have been blasphemy in the eyes of Sf fandom, it was not willful blasphemy." Aldiss himself suggested to Larry Ashmead that they "discuss whether the novel should appear as Sf or just fiction"[20]

Still, the novel is typically—or better said, topically—Aldiss. He engages such continuing themes as entropy and change; the artist; time and space, and their relationship with humanity; drugs; and the metamorphosis of humanity into something new. It begins straightforwardly enough, with narrative passages detailing Charteris' experiences. But the longer one explores the world of the novel, the more complex it becomes. Griffin notes that if *An Age* "makes a thrilling first read, *Barefoot* is better the second time around."[21] And he is correct. In spite of surface complexities, the novel is both enjoyable and stimulating.

It is also as much topographical as any of Aldiss' more conventional science-fiction novels, except that here the topography exists within the human mind as well. His map struggles to chart ways through the multi-valued perceptions endemic to "an entire culture gone hippie and yippie,"[22] the "twencen" (twentieth century) or "wesciv" (Western civilization) of the novel. In the ambiguity of Charteris and Charteris' world, we see the ambiguities of our own present and future.

Notes

[1] For an extension of Aldiss' theme, see my poem "One With Him," *Star-Line,* 6, no. 6 (November/December 1983), p. 5.

[2] Aldiss' approach here resembles Browning's "infinite moment," most fully developed in such poems as "Porphyria's Lover."

[3] Mathews, pp. 35-38; see also Griffin and Wingrove, pp. 115-117.

[4] Letter to Larry Ashmead, 5 December 1966. Huntington Library, San Marino, CA.

[5] Griffin and Wingrove, p. 111.

[6] In "Magic and Bare Boards" (*Hell's Cartographers,* p. 200), Aldiss details briefly his publishing difficulties with the novel. See also Griffin and Wingrove, pp. 141-142.

[7] Mathews, pp. 34-35. James Gunn has noted that such structural experimentation was part of the "New Wave" movement "away from traditional science fiction and toward the literary mainstream." Such experiments "at their best . . . were effective in saying what could not be said as well any other way; at their worst they were distancing, distracting, and obscure." ("A Retrospective: Science Fiction's 'New Wave,' " *Fantasy Newsletter,* 46 [March 1982], p. 12.) Griffin and Wingrove assert continually in *Apertures* that Aldiss blends science fiction and contemporary "mainstream" literature. They also suggest, however, that *RPA* owes as much to C. S. Lewis' "probability-world fantasy," *The Dark Tower,* as it does to the French anti-novelists (pp. 137-139).

[8] Greenland, p. 85.

[9] For a discussion of the characters' names, see Griffin and Wingrove, pp. 141-142.

[10] Mathews, p. 38; for a discussion of how the novel's style effects readers, see Griffin and Wingrove, pp. 136-137.

[11] Of the first fifty verbs in the novel, fewer than eighteen are active; the rest are copular, state-of-being, or active forms either negated or coupled with pseudo-passive auxiliaries or modals. The active verbs include "said," "began," "stood," and "made," which generally deny specific action.

[12] Griffin and Wingrove, p. 136.

[13] Letter to Michael R. Collings, 6 April 1984.

[14] Anthony Burgess, *Joysprick: An Introduction to the Language of James Joyce* (New York: Harcourt Brace Jovanovich, 1975), p. 48. For a discussion of Joycean language in *Barefoot*, see Griffin and Wingrove, pp. 122–126; and Greenland, "The Times Themselves Talk Nonsense: Language in *Barefoot in the Head*," *Extrapolation*, 17 (September 1979), 32–41.

[15] "Magic and Bare Boards," p. 200.

[16] Burgess (p. 45) similarly notes Joyce's use of "The Agenbite of Inwit" as a structural motif in *Ulysses*.

[17] Greenland, p. 90.

[18] Greenland, p. 89.

[19] See particularly Griffin and Wingrove, pp. 111–150, and Mathews, pp. 44–48.

[20] Greenland, p. 71; Griffin and Wingrove, p. 111; Letter to Larry Ashmead, 18 December 1968. Huntington Library, San Marino, CA.

[21] Griffin, p. 122.

[22] "Magic and Bare Boards," p. 200. In a recent letter, Aldiss wrote that "there's a real topography underlying the fictional one: the map of Europe. Much of the book was written in those places, Maastricht, etc." (Letter to Michael R. Collings, 22 January 1985).

VII
Decade the 1970s:
Frankenstein Unbound

After completing *Report on Probability A* and *Barefoot* (the latter taking nearly three years), Aldiss felt as if he had written himself out of science fiction. He turned to mainstream fiction, completing the first two Horatio Stubbs novels, *The Hand-Reared Boy* (1970) and *A Soldier Erect* (1972), both best-sellers that crystalized the essentially British experiences of a young man growing into maturity. The titles suggest the erotic directions of the novels, while the character's name evokes simultaneously such English heroic figures as Lord Nelson or the fictional Admiral Horatio Hornblower as well as the sense of a rather common, down-to-earth character—Stubbs.[1] In addition, Aldiss completed two other projects: *The Shape of Further Things* (1970), a memoir covering the time he wrote the manuscript; and *Billion Year Spree* (1973), a history of science fiction that remains both readable and informative, full of humor and personal touches that lift it above mere literary history and reflect Aldiss' personality.

The hiatus from science fiction was time well spent, for in 1973 he published one of his most remarkable books, *Frankenstein Unbound*. Aldiss enjoyed working on it; he wrote to Diane Cleaver that he was "absolutely revelling in a super, smashing, philosophical, horrific novel about Frankenstein and Mary Shelley."[2] The novel received wide critical attention: the title of Mathews' study, *Aldiss Unbound*, suggests the novel's importance in Aldiss' canon. Gillespie concludes his "Literature Which Awakens Us," with a lengthy discussion of the novel. Patrick McLeod's "Frankenstein: Unbound and Otherwise" devotes more time to Aldiss' transformation than to Shelley's original creation. And Griffin and Wingrove include a chapter on it in *Apertures*.[3] The critical responses are virtually unanimous in identifying *Frankenstein Unbound* as central to understanding Aldiss' fictions.

The novel evolved from Aldiss' research for *Billion Year Spree*, in which he argues for Shelley's *Frankenstein* as the first science-fiction novel. Her novel was complex, approaching humanity from a number of levels; but as Aldiss and others have noted, that complexity has been lost through the many transformations the "first great myth of the industrial age" has endured in books and on film:

> The monster has spawned Sons, Daughters, Ghosts, and Houses;
> has taken on Brides and created Woman; has perforce shacked up
> with Dracula and Wolf Man; has enjoyed Evil, Horror, and Re-

venge, and has even had the Curse; on one occasion, it met Abbott and Costello.

The monster is now a stock character, imitated and diminished, its original horror replaced by "febrile fantasies of shock and giggles."[4]

Aldiss restores much of the monster's mythic complexity, then reaches beyond to include Mary Shelley herself, integrating materials inherited from her nineteenth-century Gothic tradition with twentieth-century promises and threats. To help explain, Aldiss' achievement in *Frankenstein Unbound*, Griffin refers to Ezra Pound's five modes of criticism: discussion in prose, translation, exercise in a particular style, musical rendition, and new composition. Aldiss approaches Shelley through at least three: by direct criticism in *BYS*, by incorporating her stylistic devices into his prose, and by new composition. "Aldiss is not attempting simply to rewrite the original without its flaws," Griffin continues, "but to reinterpret it from our modern perspective."[5] To this end, Aldiss re-examines two of Shelley's original themes—man's confrontation with himself, and the disintegration of society resulting from man's "arrogation of power,"[6] applying these themes to the contemporary world.

Frankenstein Unbound suggests earlier novels, of course. The initial catastrophe which divorces Joe Bodenland from his own time and space results from human irresponsibility in detonating nuclear devices in Earth orbits, reminiscent of the Accident in *Greybeard*. Aldiss explores the ambiguities of time and space, as he had done in *An Age, RPA,* and *Barefoot.* The format recalls both Shelley's epistolary narrative and the observational stance of *RPA*. The novel reflects Aldiss' continuing concerns—yet it does much more. By relying on Shelley's original, he comments on the nature of science and twentieth-century life and on the effects of scientific imagination on our world. At the same time, the novel seems intensely personal, with strong connections between Shelley and Aldiss leading one critic to assert that when Bodenland "makes love to Mary Shelley, we sense a wish-fulfillment for Aldiss."[7]

Frankenstein Unbound begins as a straightforward science-fiction adventure. On August 20, 2020, Joe Bodenland writes a letter to his wife Mina—the date simultaneously sets the novel in the future while emphasizing the "twentieth" century[8]; Mina's name, on the other hand, evokes the Gothic tradition of Bram Stoker. In the letter, Bodenland defines the catastrophe by quoting a headline: "SPACE/TIME RUPTURES, SCIENTISTS SAY" (Part I, Ch. 1). Bodenland, we discover, is an observer; as a former Presidential advisor, he has access to spy devices through which he watches his grandchildren at play. Their actions, he concludes, are "in this world of madness . . . the only significant activity" (Pt. I, Ch. 1). Soon, however, Boden observes scenes that transcend mere activities; and here, unlike his strategies in *RPA* and *Barefoot,* Aldiss provides keys to interpretations.

The children bury a scooter, an act which reverberates throughout the novel, not only as Bodenland recounts the episode for the entertain-

41

ment of Byron and Shelley in the Switzerland of 1816, but also when he realizes his own position in a society that has transformed humans into machines (Part II, Ch. 25). The passage blends the Aldissian image of observer immured behind his banks of mechanical eyes with an allusion to Wells' *The Time Machine,* with its subterranean machinery and monstrous Morlocks in counterpoint to the flower-garden world of the Eloi. As the novel continues, Bodenland discovers that his own time, like that of Wells' Eloi or Shelley's monster, was an illusion hiding futility and death.[9] He is as much a victim of illusion as any of Aldiss' earlier heroes. and the novel details the systematic stripping away of those illusions as Bodenland replaces them with a more dangerous assumption—that he is to be equated with Frankenstein's monster. His separation from humanity is foreshadowed early in the opening chapter. He becomes so involved in observing his grandchildren that he gives up all work and becomes a static observer, their actions now "inscrutable" to him.

As the children's ritual continues, they mound flowers over the grave of the buried machinery, then begin a spontaneous chant that borrows the dead forms of Christianity but is devoid of meaning. The chant leads to dance, an "instinctual celebration of their own physical health" (Part I, Ch. 1) and continues until the boy innocently exposes himself to one of the girls; "She made some comment, smiling, and that was that." Bodenland is enough of a man of letters to recognize the mythic elements in the children's activities, which he places in opposition to the power of intellect: "They live in myth. Under the onslaught of school, intellect will break in—crude robber intellect—and myth will wither and die like the bright flowers on their mysterious grave" (Part I, Ch. 1). And yet, he continues, there is one overriding mythic pattern that retains its strength in spite of the intellect: the Myth of Progress, that "ever-increasing production and industrialization will bring the greatest happiness for the greatest number all around the globe" (Part I, Ch. 1). This myth structures Bodenland's life and provides the subject for Aldiss' scrutiny in the novel. Even the wording—"greatest happiness for the greatest number"—echoes Benthamite philosophical pragmatism, directing the reader toward the early nineteenth century, when most of the novel takes place.

This opening chapter not only allows Aldiss to manipulate recurrent patterns in his own prose, but also establishes critical patterns in Bodenland's imagination. The dance, coupled with the promise of sexuality, recurs twice in the novel. Quite literally in the center of the book, Bodenland meets Mary Shelley. They talk of her future influence as a writer, and their discussion culminates in their making love. Theirs is a celebration of spirit and flesh, concluding with what Bodenland refers to as a "formal dance." This experience establishes the first connections between Bodenland and the world into which he has been thrown. Significantly, the chapter ends with the two lovers speaking the name that brought them together—*Frankenstein* (Part II, Ch. 9).

The dance image repeats near the end of the novel. Frankenstein has brought a female monster to life; the male takes her outside, into the snow beneath the tower of Frankenstein's secret laboratory. There, in the moon-light (There are two moons!) and beneath the voyeuristic eyes of Boden-land, they dance "like two lunatic children" (Pt. II, Ch. 22). Earlier, children had been seen as sane in a world essentially mad; now, after Bodenland has become acculturated into the worlds of Shelley and of Frankenstein, after he has become aware of himself as child-product of the same imaginations which created the monsters, the dance becomes threatening. The first dance culminated in the promise of sexuality—Tony simply shows his penis and Doreen smiles. The second culminated in an archtypally "Romantic" encounter, with Bodenland and the mistress of Percy Shelley making love, speaking of spirits and infinity, of phantoms and wild imaginings.

In the final sequence, however, there are no illusions. Through a major timeslip, Mary Wollstonecraft Godwin has disappeared from Bodenland's Europe. He confronts Frankenstein, intent upon killing the monster, and observes the mating dance of the monsters. Aldiss includes a number of echoes from the first dance: there is a grave, for instance, the tower in which Bodenland will soon kill Frankenstein and at the heart of which lie the machines that created the monsters' artificial life. Instead of flowers and warmth, however, Bodenland sees only snow and cold and desolation. It is night; the two moons glow like eyes, symbolizing the irresponsible meddling of science in his own time that has altered the space–time con-tinuum. He watches the creations of the archtypal scientist/meddler, Frankenstein (himself the creation of Mary Shelley, the first science-fiction writer). The monsters dance, but he sees no beauty, just mimic flight and pursuit. The female's face is bestial rather than human; wolves howl accompaniment to their movements; and their coupling is both brief and brutal, as far unlike his own coupling with Mary Shelley as that was from Tony's innocently exposing himself to Doreen's curiosity. Bodenland has transformed from civilized observer surrounded by the material luxuries of his time to monster intent upon destruction. The love-making of the monsters leaves him "dry of mouth, sick at heart," irrevocably distanced from his first views of such a dance in chapter one.

This shift in Bodenland's attitudes is critical since he represents our century. Through his first name, he suggests commonplace humanity. But his last name inverts that suggestion. Boden—the German word for "floor," "ground," or "soil"—suggests stability, doubly so when connected with "land." The irony is that Bodenland enjoys no stability. In his own time and space, he is subject to timeslips, the final one carrying him beyond recognizable time. He becomes a wanderer, pursuing the fleeing monsters.

Simultaneously, however, he is a creation, analogous to Frankenstein's monster. Bodenland refers to Shelley's work as the "first novel of the Scientific Revolution" (Part II, Ch. 6) and to himself and his time as "heirs to the gifts of Frankenstein" (Part II, Ch. 12). Byron and Shelley rhapsodize over the future of humanity as it progresses through techno-logical and industrial stages toward social equality and utopian peace. Bodenland disagrees with them, yet in his disagreement recognizes the myths about progress that had shaped the twentieth and twenty-first centuries; Bodenland's own society was literally a product of the romantic imagination. Twice, as he discusses the true state of future societies, characters ask him whether the future is to be peopled with Frankenstein's monsters (Part II, Chs. 8, 17).

The answer to this question, as Bodenland finally realizes, is "Yes." The future belongs to a humanity limited by the nineteenth-century imagination to a static conception of time, to "organized science" allied with business and government with no interest in the individual—"Its meat was statistics! It was death to the spirit" (Part II, Ch. 19). The Frankenstein mentality succeeded, initiating the irresponsible meddling with natural forces that resulted in timeslips and the possible end of humanity. Even worse, the suggestions of machinery in the first chapter have now developed into full threats. The technological culture Bodenland has known is defined as a monster's body, bereft of spirit. Immediately after Bodenland reaches this conclusion, he sees the monster's face for the first time and is astounded by the beauty in it. It is not the hideous patch-work face of the horror films, but a face like a painted helmet, a creature that looks "lathe-turned" (Part II, Ch. 19).

At this point, Bodenland becomes the true "Frankenstein's monster" of the novel, a co-creation (with the original monster) of Mary Shelley and Victor Frankenstein. The monster is articulate, logical and morally neutral; Bodenland surrenders to the animal within himself (a part of human nature Frankenstein accurately describes earlier in the novel). Bodenland, not the monster, kills Frankenstein, then sets out to destroy the monsters, tracking them through icy lands, just as in the opening chapters of Shelley's novel Frankenstein pursues *his* monster. Incapable of fully understanding the message he has discovered, Bodenland *becomes* the message Aldiss wishes to communicate. In a moment of ironic perception, Bodenland speaks of innumerable alternate universes resulting from the timeslips, including a "2020 in which I exist merely as a character in a novel about Frankenstein and Mary" (Part II, Ch. 24), a supposition truer than he knows.

This confusion of character with "reality" is equally critical to the novel. Aldiss knows the difficulties in writing a narrative in which a man from the future, Byron, Shelley, Mary Godwin, Victor Frankenstein, his fiancée Elizabeth, and his monster-creation all appear. Aldiss does not allow Mary Shelley to meet her fictional creations; Bodenland mediates between them. Gillespie notes that

> Bodenland has entered a world which is fictional, and he has taken Mary into a world where her fiction has "come true." But what is now fiction? Surely the twentieth century is a fiction invented by its imaginative ancestors. Frankenstein's landscape of 1816 was a fiction invented by Mary, and is now a fiction in the mind of Brian Aldiss. Yet there was an actual world of 1816, without which Brian Aldiss and the world of 2020 could never

44

have existed. And an assumption of that world was that Man could discover the secrets of nature in order to make a better world. The process of progress had started already in England. Those people were responsible for the world ahead of them. But, even in 2020, Bodenland still believes in the fallacy of progress.[10]

This layering of reality upon reality (and Gillespie does not refer to the final layer, the reader who enters the imagination of Brian Aldiss through the fictional transcriptions of a twenty-first-century man's journal of his travels in time and space) is precisely what we have come to expect from Aldiss. And within that complexity, Aldiss embeds a statement about the relationship of Mary Shelley's Frankenstein to our own age.

Mathews concludes that in *Frankenstein Unbound*, for the first time since *Earthworks*, a character ends the novel "in control of things, in possession of a consciousness beyond the cycle of head and heart. Both have been swallowed up in action as [Bodenland], like Prometheus, commands fire to change the world. We leave Bodenland stranded in time and heroic; and he reaches us past the time-slips—*we have his report.*"[11] Although this conclusion captures the sense of power at the end of the novel, it seems overstated. In one sense at least, *we* are as fictional as Bodenland, since we are the intended audience for fictional transcripts. And, while the conclusion is highly mythic, there seems little indication that Bodenland is in control. He followed the monsters, bringing his nuclear-powered armored car with him. Then he discarded that remnant of his own time, to pursue the monsters on foot through frozen wastes, past ghostly spires of cathedrals and castles, into the unknown, where he finally sights the monsters as they approach the gates of an enormous city. At the last possible moment, he fires, first killing the female, then the male as it races toward him. The sense of control, however, passes from Bodenland—now the gun-wielding monster obsessed with murder—and to the monster, who alone understands that he and Bodenland are more alike than different. Both are creations—and the monster is in fact superior to Bodenland, having known and practiced compassion. The monster's final words become an *envoi* to the novel:

> This I will tell you, and through you, all men, if you are deemed fit to rejoin your kind: that my death will weigh more heavily upon you than my life. No fury I might possess could be a match for yours. Moreover, though you seek to bury me, yet will you continuously resurrect me! Once I am unbound, I am unbounded (Part II, Ch. 37).

Bodenland shoots, killing the monster. Yet his own end—the "resolution" to the "novel" he is transcribing onto his recorder—remains ambiguous and obscure. He crouches outside the enormous city, half-fearful, half-challenging. He is alone on the ice; in the distance lights die in a city as static and emblematic as Malacia. Bodenland remains alone, waiting in the darkness. Gillespie refers to the ironic conclusion of the novel; we experience Bodenland's tragedy, not the monster's, since by pursuing the monster Bodenland has "extinguished his own humanity," destroying that which he has been seeking throughout."[12]

This concluding image raises a curious note. While Aldiss clearly modeled his tale on Shelley's *Frankenstein*, he also suggests her later novel, *The Last Man*. He discusses this novel in a critical article, citing William Walling's claim that by "interweaving the themes of isolation and the end of civilization," Shelley "creates a prophetic account of modern industrial society, in which the creative personality becomes more and more alienated."[13] This is, of course, also precisely what Aldiss has created in his novel. Bodenland is incrementally isolated, initially within his own society, and finally from it. In the world of 1816, even his retreat to Mary Shelley is denied him when she "slips" away. If she had not disappeared, his murdering Frankenstein would have made him too corrupt for her presence. Eventually his world narrows to the two monsters fleeing before him: at the end, he destroys even them, leaving himself alone. Like *Frankenstein* (in terms of plot chronology, at least, since Shelley's fable begins at the end, with Frankenstein chasing the monster across the ice), *Frankenstein Unbound* concludes with a vigil in the snow. But even more like *The Last Man,* it concludes with the disintegration and extinction of human society—Shelley's novel through a world-wide plague, Aldiss' through scientific meddling and irresponsibility in 2020. Bodenland is "the last man" since he (and as represented by him, his generation) has destroyed all else.

If *Frankenstein Unbound* is an "unabashed tribute" to Mary Shelley, it simultaneously attains a wider perspective. Aldiss has not only borrowed from Shelley's most famous book, but also from her last novel, *The Last Man,* to create a novel which reaffirms the horror of Shelley's original and then transcends it, focusing Frankenstein, his monster, and Mary Shelley into a statement directed at our own world and our own society.

Notes

[1] In line with Aldiss' interest in art, *Stubbs* also suggests an English painter, George Stubbs (Letter to Michael R. Collings, 22 January 1985).

[2] Letter to Diane Cleaver, 15 September 1972. Huntington Library, San Marino, CA.

[3] McLeod, "Frankenstein: Unbound and Otherwise," *Extrapolation,* 21 (1981), 158–166.

[4] McLeod, p. 158: citing *Billion Year Spree* (New York: Schocken, 1974), p. 23f.

[5] Griffin and Wingrove, p. 105.

[6] *BYS,* p. 27; Gillespie traces these themes through *Non-Stop, Greybeard,* and *Barefoot.*

[7] McLeod, pp. 162–163.

[8] Mathews, p. 51.

[9] This image is fully explored in Aldiss' "Where the Lines Converge" (1977),

a novella about static observers, banks of cameras, and the impact of technology on life. The allusion to Wells is also important, since Aldiss was involved with Wells' works at the time. His 1965 award-winning story "The Saliva Tree" was a Wellsian pastiche; and his next novel (unpublished until 1980) applied the techniques of *Frankenstein Unbound* to Wells' *Island of Dr. Moreau,* although less successfully.

[10] Gillespie, pp. 183–184.

[11] Mathews, p. 54.

[12] Gillespie, p. 185.

[13] "Mary Wollstonecraft Shelley," in *Science Fiction Writers,* ed. E. F. Bleiler (New York: Scribners, 1982), p. 8. While Aldiss was not consciously aware at the time of connections between *Frankenstein Unbound* and *The Last Man,* he has since noted that the "suggestion that the end of *Unbound* echoes Mary Shelley's Last Man . . . feels right" (Letter to Michael Collings, 7 September 1983).

VIII

Decade the 1970s:
The Eighty-Minute Hour and *The Malacia Tapestry*

In 1974, Aldiss published *Space Opera*, a collection of stories by Edmond Hamilton, Leigh Brackett, Isaac Asimov, Ray Bradbury, Philip K. Dick, and others. In his introduction, Aldiss differentiates between science fiction and space opera. The former is "a big muscular horny creature, with a mass of bristling antennae and proprioceptors on its skull"; the latter, "a gentle creature with red lips and a dash of stardust in her hair. . . . Science fiction is for real. Space opera is for fun. Generally."

It isn't surprising, then, that Aldiss' *The Eighty-Minute Hour: A Space Opera* (1975) is an exercise in humor, exaggeration, and hilarious coincidence, with a touch of screwy ideas. While working on the novel, Aldiss referred to it as "simple (almost simple) space opera" with "nothing obscure about it at all, just a jolly chunk of space opera."[1] Perhaps better than any of his other works, *EMH* suggests the depths of Aldiss' humor. Greenland has noted that nothing in the "encroaching horror" of *Frankenstein Unbound* foreshadows the effervescence of *EMH*, with its cast of outrageous characters, including Devlin Carnate, Choggles Chaplain, Glamis Fevertree, Dinah Sorbutt, Monty Zoomer, and Attica Saigon Smix. David Wingrove counters this argument, calling the novel "a theatrical comedy with all of space/time as its stage" in which

> The plentiful songs, the hilarious and fanciful exaggerations, the bizarre coincidences and a grotesque proliferation of all kinds of artificial life forms are counter-balanced by the sinister, and, at times, apocalyptic visions of the disintegration of society. It is perhaps Aldiss' funniest book and, at times, his most cutting. The humour is dark and reminiscent, within the genre, of the work of Kurt Vonnegut and John Sladek, as well as Philip K. Dick.[2]

Instead of a United Nations, we have the Dissident Nations. As one character says about finding the Koh-i-nor diamond washed ashore in France, "It was incredible. . . . But I expect incredible things" (Ch. 1). Aldiss abruptly shifts scenery, landscapes, and characters, even perceptions of reality. Characters find themselves

> . . . walking through suite after suite of interconnecting rooms, each bigger than the previous one, until the ultimate room of the series encompassed all the others and they were forced to turn about and seek another way (Ch. 1).

One of the characters, Julian, comments that he "knew this entire castle as a lad," which Aldiss immediately undercuts by having Julian add: "Spent my entire adolescence trying to find my way out of it" (Ch. 1). Throughout, Aldiss paints expected stereotypes, then re-touches them with a comic brush, creating simultaneously space opera and caricature. Mathews calls the novel an extended definition of Dusty Sykes' "slouch humor" from *Greybeard*—humor which "doesn't make you laugh out loud, but it slouches through the grand issues and themes of all Aldiss' work, 'slouching towards Bethlehem to be born.'"[3] On occasion, the novel does make one laugh out loud; it is a kaleidoscope of puns, inversions (both linguistic and situational), and games based on conventional space opera. It explores and expands them, much as *RPA* expanded narrative conventions or *Barefoot* explored language and style. Here, as before, Aldiss pushes the edges of a genre as far as they can go, often breaking through to new forms. Carrying the phrase "space opera" to logical extremes, he concludes Chapter 10 with a duet in lyric verse. Other characters break into song as the novel progresses, including an operatic trio (Ch. 27) and the requisite "happy ending," complete with sextet and interspersed choruses (Ch. 34). Aldiss may have initially envisioned a "simple" space opera, but on its own grounds, *EMH* is as multivalued as *Barefoot*, the result of Aldiss' having worked it "all over a dozen times" before its complexities were fully realized.[4] It is, however, a complexity tempered by Aldiss' wit unleashed, exploding across his chosen stage.

From *EMH*, with its futuristic settings and layerings of games and puns, Aldiss moves to the boundaries between two other genres, science fiction and fantasy. His transition from *EMH* to *The Malacia Tapestry* (1976) reasserts his mastery over language and style. The first-person, straight-line narrative of *MT* is deceptively simple, yet entirely appropriate for the sense of psuedo-Renaissance picaresque adventure Aldiss creates. The main character, Perian de Chirolo, is equally deceptive. Like Joe Bodenland, he understands little of what surrounds him, but in living through the episodes which form *MT*, he exemplifies Aldiss' themes.

The novel is "about" many things: time and space; entropy, stasis, and change; art and the artist and their relationships to life; reality and illusion; light, shadow, and the reflection of light; progress and degeneration. Aldiss had pursued these themes for two decades, but here they appear in a new, slightly puzzling dress. Patrick Parrinder refers to the novel as an example of the difficulty of defining science fiction. There is no doubt, he assures us, of Aldiss' mastery in *MT*; it is "an exercise in deliberate fantasy." Parrinder catalogues fantastic elements, including a feudal city–state in a parallel universe; astrologers, wizards, and magic; and flying humans, satyrs, and other strange creatures. The result "is an entertaining, quasi-historical extravaganza which was not published under the science-fiction category." On the other hand, he continues, there is much about the novel that is science fiction: alternate evolution with *homo saurus* descended from not-quite-extinct dinosaurs; a neo-utopian city within a neo-Byzantine empire; and, most curious of all, a narrative sequence in which fantastic engravings by G. B. Tiepolo become "realistic illustrations." Like Heinlein's *Stranger in a Strange Land* or McCaffrey's dragon novels, Malacia remains ambivalent, divided between history, fantasy, and science fiction.[5] De Chirolo's world resembles our conception of Renaissance society: Vesuvius is a favorite topic for painters; scholars investigate the eating habits of Philip of Macedon and quote Aristotle; gardens boast of mandrills imported from Africa; and the city is threatened by an Ottoman army, some time after the death of the great Suleiman. Yet into this sense of historicity, Aldiss intrudes the fantastic. The world of Malacia blends art and nature, illusion and reality, just as the novel itself does, at least for the first third of the text.

Then Aldiss shifts. We discover that Malacia is not of this Earth at all, but of an alternate reality in which monotheism is as heretical as the belief that humanity descended from apes (Book I, Ch. 2). God, Satan, and Minerva control the world, separating its inhabitants into constantly warring factions. In a monumental work-in-progress, *Disquisitions on Disquisitions,* de Chirolo's father speculates that at the battle of Itssobeshiquetzilaha, over 3,175,000 years before, saurians might have been defeated and Malacia subsequently ruled by another possible "human" race—including, presumably, a mammalian one. The hot-blooded Perian de Chirolo and his lusty companions in fact descend from the cold-blooded saurians they ceremonially hunt. For all its apparent historicity, and in spite of its fantastic elements, Malacia is not of our world, but something essentially alien. The novel is as ambiguous as *The Joyous Tragedy of the Prince and Patricia and General Gerald and Jemima* (also referred to as a "doleful comedy"), the play whose creation covers most of *MT*'s four-hundred pages. And it is entirely appropriate that the play, recorded by an invention called the "Zahnoscope," is neither produced nor seen during the novel.

Into this complex structuring of history, fantasy, and science fiction, Aldiss weaves his themes, the most important being the interplay of entropy, stasis, and change. Malacia suffers under an "Original Curse," that the city should remain forever unchanged, with time "congealing" around it (to use de Chirolo's term). The city's governors avoid change. De Chirolo's involvement with Otto Bengtsohn's innovative zahnoscope opposes him to the forces of stasis, particularly since the device is potentially not only an art form but an instrument for revolution and change as well. Interwoven with de Chirolo's sexual escapades are scenes in which he poses for the Zahnoscope, becoming drawn into a scheme to change society. The Original Curse disallows such change, however; Bengtsohn is arrested and executed, while de Chirolo's involvement deprives him of his goal of marrying into the wealthy Hoytola family. Throughout, characters discuss change, plot change, act (although diffidently) to create change—yet nothing changes. One of the principal characters, Bedelar, suggests that perhaps their world is ending, not through cataclysm, but through having ordinary events happen more slowly until life simply ceases. "Like a clock stopping," another character responds. "More like a tapestry," Bedelar says. "Things might run down and never move again, so that we and everything would hang there like a tapestry in the air for ever more" (Book I, Ch. 1).

Di Chirolo contemplates the image of the tapestry, but not deeply enough. In spite of his talk and his ambitions, he cannot change. His final appearance in the novel parallels his first; he, like all of Malacia, is merely a thread in a recurring tapestry of unchanging time.[6] During a vision in a forest, de Chirolo confronts a wizard who confirms that de Chirolo's life repeats "an endless fiction." The Original Curse that envelops Malacia binds de Chirolo as well (Book II, Ch. 4).

De Chirolo is an actor, an artist, like many of his friends—musicians, dancers, painters. Through such characters, *MT* confronts the role and nature of art, the "Uncomfortable Pause Between Life and Art," to borrow the title of Aldiss' 1969 short story. Life and art oppose the specter of stasis and time, holding up their creations against the measure of reality. The novel begins with art imitating life; then art merges with life as de Chirolo impersonates an ancient painting by a forgotten artist, transforming the visual image into a theatrical costume; and finally life itself imitates art. De Chirolo notes of a puppet show by the Great Harino that "Most amazing was the way in which one soon accepted the puppets for reality, and the screen for life, as if there were no others!" (Book II, Ch. 3).

At this point, the treatment of stasis and change intersects with that of art. The complications in *MT* arise from and parallel de Chirolo's role as General Gerald in *Mendicula,* a highly traditional play of love and deceit, betrayal and despair. Throughout the novel, de Chirolo rails against the play as representing only the past and therefore being inappropriate for audiences of his own time. Yet, we learn, Bengtsohn selected the play to record on the zahnoscope for precisely that reason. Its traditionality would mask the revolutionary technique of its presentation through a series of photographic slides. He uses convention against itself to produce change. De Chirolo cannot accept this, ambitious as he is to introduce change into his own life, and argues against the play—the unbelievable actions; the shallow, self-serving characters; the paucity of imagination that produced it originally.

In spite of the straight-line narrative technique Aldiss uses, however, by the end of the novel he has introduced increasingly ambiguous layerings of complexity and meaning, as art imitates reality, which in turn imitates art. The play was chosen by Bengtsohn because it touched human motivations understandable over millenia: yet the readers gradually discover that in spite of de Chirolo's objections to it as facile and superficial, it reflects his own life. Episodes in the novel suggest the static photographs the zahnoscope produces—characters do not seem to move, but simply are, like the Holman Hunt painting of shepherd and maiden in

RPA. De Chirolo himself reflects the archtypal model recurrent throughout Malacian history and art—and he has no more life, no deeper self than the shallow character he personates.

There is, however, an even more devastating irony. It would be bad enough for de Chirolo to discover that his love for the aristocratic Armida follows the unchanging pattern of ancient drama; it is worse to discover that the play itself is little more than an illusion. The slides are judged subversive by the Council and destroyed. Even though their production has provided a connecting thread for the novel, they are destroyed before any of the main characters see the finished result. The slides simply cease to exist—they are ultimately meaningless. And so is de Chirolo within the stasis of Malacia. His life recapitulates the doleful comedy and joyous tragedy of *Mendicula,* which in turn reflect Malacia's Original Curse.

The final episodes of *MT* confirm its primary concern—stasis. De Chirolo ends up in the arms of a woman, not unusual for him; but the scene is important precisely because nothing has changed, because Malacia will not change. Artists will continue to grapple with time, taking longer to produce fewer works—or, in the case of the muralist Nicholas Fatember, who becomes obsessed with the impossibility of art fully reproducing life, producing no art at all, in spite of his being the premier painter of his time. Artistic creativity, like life itself, slows, diminishes, dies as the entropic nature of Malacia's Original Curse asserts itself.

For a long novel, *MT* is curiously static, mimicking theme through plot. De Chirolo's love affairs are short, mild, rather superficial, except for his grand passion for Armida—itself more theatrical than real, as events prove. The few catastrophes allow for easy resolution. The Ottoman army surrounds Malacia, but a few plague-ridden bodies dropped from Bengtsohn's experimental balloons rout them. De Chirolo is hailed as a hero for his part in the engagement—for having ridden a horse strapped to a platform beneath the lead balloon. He receives the city's acclamation for doing literally nothing. Bengtsohn's revolutionary plans center on *Mendicula,* a play frozen in time and space; yet the play is destroyed unseen. Beds become indistinguishable; lovers shift from one to another without regard for more than minimal formalities. The single "heroic" action of the novel—de Chirolo's dispatching of an allosaurus—takes fewer than two pages to narrate.

The novel is indeed a tapestry, intricate and complex, with wit and humor enough to replicate a Renaissance world. Its characters are varied and eccentric, its locales exotic and lush: castles and palaces; formal gardens and wild, romantically sublime groves. It represents an entire culture, static and unchanging except as it devolves toward entropy and final motionlessness. The technological and social progress darkly imagined in *Frankenstein Unbound* (and with more terrifying consequences) is revealed as merely a myth. One may speak of it and perhaps talk oneself into longing for it, but never achieve it. Quite the opposite—neither artistic achievement, nor the quality of food, nor the state of gardens and villas (and family fortunes), nor the numbers of ancestral animals available

52

for slaughter during ritual hunts—nothing is quite what it was long ago in Malacia. In the image of the tapestry, Aldiss creates a variant on the Holman Hunt painting critical to so many of his fictions. Only in this instance, we perceive in reverse; we are invited *into* that static moment itself.

The opposite movement occurs in a mirror-piece to *MT*, Aldiss' long poem *Pile: Petals from St Klaed's Computer* (1979). The poem is illustrated by Mike Wilks, whose finely detailed renderings of the unchanging city of Pile highlight Aldiss' text. In the poem, the Lord Scart, disturbed by his inability to defeat his enemies, approaches "The Blessed St Klaed's computer" to plead for his enemies' destruction, even at the cost of Pile itself. The computer agrees; Pile is destroyed by earthquake and flood, and Scart descends into the "ulterior Water-world," a counterpoint to Pile. There Lord Scart, "embodiment of the integration of art and science," according to David Wingrove, "goes through the mirror of self down into the depths of his own primordial self, to throw off the cluttering paraphernalia of civilization as made manifest in the abominable city."[7] Monochromatic Pile ceases to exist; in its place Scart enters a fantasy wilderness of pastel color (the only color plate in the book), and "Thus one more psyche to the bright world came."

Pile is a wildly funny poem, with intricately rhyming lines that create impelling rhythms. It shows Aldiss' considerable skills as a poet, coupled with his carefully developed sense of plot and character. It is short, where *MT* is long; it ends in total change and discovery of self, where *MT* ends in stasis and self-deceit. Taken together, however, the two illuminate two perspectives within the unity of Aldiss' vision.

Notes

[1] Letter to Larry Ashmead, 1 August 1972; Letter to Larry Ashmead, 10 January 1973. Huntington Library, San Marino, CA.

[2] Greenland, p. 70; Griffin and Wingrove, p. 174.

[3] Mathews, pp. 54–55.

[4] Letter to Larry Ashmead, 5 June 1973. Huntington Library, San Marino, CA.

[5] Patrick Parrinder, *Science Fiction: Its Criticism and Its Teaching* (London: Methuen, 1980), pp. 3, 25–29. Aldiss notes an even closer parallel with Nabokov's *Ada*, which also transposes time and place (Letter to Michael R. Collings, 22 January 1985).

[6] In spite of arguments by Griffin and Wingrove (p. 219), Greenland (p. 75), and others that de Chirolo displays greater maturity at the end of the novel, it is possible to find a number of exact parallels—verbal, syntactic, situational, imagistic, structural, and episodic—between the opening pages of *MT* and the last, suggesting that there is indeed little or no progression or development in the plot, in the society of Malacia, or in the personality and character of Perian de Chirolo. In a discussion of the novel during the International Conference on the Fantastic (March 21, 1984), Aldiss noted that he intended to downplay as much as possible the sense of movement and development in the novel.

[7] Griffin and Wingrove, pp. 230–231.

IX

Decade the 1970s:
Brothers of the Head and
Enemies of the System

In a letter to Larry Ashmead in 1968, Aldiss described what he perceived as the state of western society:

> It's a curious climate over here at present—people very uneasy, with devaluation and now the withdrawals from Singapore, etc.; suddenly it's as if we hardly knew the world. The next few years look as if they could be tough. It seems the States also has similar feelings of unease over Vietnam. With that, and with de Gaulle ruling with his dead hands in Europe, it seems as if the western world is in for a crisis of confidence or something similarly uncomfortable.[1]

This image of a "crisis of confidence" became more central to his novels in the late 1970s, continuing into the 1980s with *Life in the West* and *Helliconia*. An early dissection of that crisis, however, occurs in the intriguingly titled novella *Brothers of the Head* (1977). If *MT* is one of Aldiss' longest and most complex novels, *Brothers* is, in its conciseness, among his most powerful.[2] On the surface, the story of the brief musical careers of Siamese twins, Tom and Barry Howe, represents one of Aldiss' most penetrating and enigmatic landscapes.

One might assume from the title that *Brothers of the Head* continues Aldiss' themes from *Barefoot in the Head*,[3] but the latter defines an inner landscape of perception altered by hallucinatory drugs, while the former has objectified the inner landscape of perception and views it externally, without the intervening veil of drugs. "Landscape" is a particularly apt word to describe this novel, which begins with an evocation of place, L'Estrange Head, where the Howe twins live. The title of the novel refers to the Howes, while simultaneously emphasizing Aldiss' treatment of humanity divided against itself.[4] The Howes are not simply Siamese twins joined at shoulder and hip; a third head, an unconscious, aged-looking head grows from Barry's shoulders, reminiscent of Rachel and Mrs. Grales in Walter Miller's *A Canticle for Leibowitz*.[5] Aldiss' triad symbolizes three levels common in contemporary psychology—the intellect, the emotions, and the dreaming subconscious. Tom is fair-haired and rational; Barry, dark and ill-tempered; and the head, for most of the story, somnolent. *Brothers of the Head* works through multiple—and often conflicting—narratives to define the conflict among the three for dominance.

54

Aldiss' next novel, *Enemies of the System,* looks at the threat of technologically induced uniformity in human society; *Brothers of the Head* relates more to isolation. The opening pages describe L'Estrange Head, a name alluded to four times in five lines to emphasize its implicit puns. There is a "strange head," both in the headland and in the head growing from Barry's shoulder; and both are estranged, isolated from the larger world.

Throughout, Aldiss suggests that the outer landscape mirrors the inner.[6] The Headland is neither true headland nor true island—it lies between them, unable to participate fully in either, an image reminiscent of Matthew Arnold's "two worlds, one dead,/ The other powerless to be born."[7] The twins are likewise insular while connected by a maze of tissue. To determine the legal status of the Headland, a character says, one would have to determine whether its system of marshes and creeks link it to or divide it from the mainland, just as one must decide whether the flesh divides or joins the Howes. They are three individuals, yet symbolically, physically, and psychically they are one, embodying the theological suggestion of trinity within unity in a world without a sense of God. At varying times, each gains control of their common body, only to lose it.

Other imagery in the novel supports Aldiss' concern about an increasingly critical sense of isolation in western culture. Religion has devolved into social organizations, paralleled externally by the decay and ruin of L'Estrange Abbey and by Laura Ashworth's history as the daughter of a contemporary Anglican clergyman who ultimately leaves the church. The Church fails both Laura and her father, as it has failed society in general.

The animal life on the Headland also helps define the twins' development since Aldiss refers to them as wild things and savage beasts. The waters of the headland become poisoned, killing the wildlife just as its isolation has in effect killed the twins. Their tragedy is foreshadowed in the ruin of nature itself; the weather turns hot, accompanied by drought, killing the Howe's retriever, Hope. The twins revert to animals, running naked through the desolation. They are described as feral, a "minotaur," a "four-legged beast." Their internal dissent forces them into a continuous state of warfare, each pummeling the other, trying to gain dominance.

As a result, Barry's heart fails, as hearts fail throughout the narrative. Tom's heart is too weak to serve both bodies, and Barry's head suffers brain damage. An artificial heart is implanted, but Tom is still linked to two unconscious heads and must consciously manipulate two bodies. Then, in the final chapter, Tom has three symbolic dreams, each preparing the reader for the awakening of the head and the final struggle for control. The message of the third head, says Wingrove, is that in suppressing our animal natures, as Barry has succeeded in doing, we awaken the "violent, uncontrolled" forces of the subconscious. "The movement of Modern Man towards nuclear war," he continues, drawing a perhaps too specific moral, "is thus seen in a new light. As ever in Aldiss, microcosm reflects macrocosm."[8] The third head uses Barry's body to try to strangle Tom, and the twins/triplets (at this point, clear definitions fail) rush from the house and disappear into the barrenness of L'Estrange Head. Unseen, they battle for control. Tom wins, but only by dying, a Pyrrhic victory.

For all of its brevity, *Brothers of the Head* is powerful, imaginative, and meticulously developed. Beneath Aldiss' parable of the human psyche lie attitudes toward art and reality—particularly when the twins incorporate the title of Aldiss' short story, "Year by Year the Evil Gains," into their songs. It touches on entropy, as old values disappear, to be replaced by a "suspension of life" (Ch. 5). And the narrative again exploits the potentials in language for multiple meaning and ambiguity. The novel looks backward, alluding to the Frankenstein mythos, and forward, with references to the Marxism and capitalism of *Enemies of the System.* Finally, it leaves the reader dissatisfied—in the best possible way. There must be more to life than this, one feels; but what? The question drives the reader back to the psychological landscape of the narrative, searching for clues to an answer that is finally as elusive as the lives of Barry, Tom, and the other. Everyone around them observes and reports, presuming to "explain" the twins, who never speak directly for themselves. Their greatest moments—and their worst—go unrecorded, yet live through the narrative, if only in the imaginations of the readers.

Enemies of the System, Aldiss writes, "was a response to openly made Soviet boasts that no western writer would depict an Earth on which Communism prevailed everywhere. They claimed that no publisher would publish it. I went one better and showed . . . whole solar system[s] under Communist rule."[9] The novel is a thought experiment, in which representatives of utopian socialist humanity, a million-year-old species called *homo uniformis* ("man alike throughout"), vacation on an untamed planet. The name of the planet, Lysenka II, suggests Aldiss' concentration of Soviet backgrounds and his attitudes toward Soviet society. By naming his world after the infamous misdirector of modern Russian biological studies, Aldiss simultaneously prefigures the effects of the visitors' experiences and satirizes Soviet pretensions in the physical as well as the social sciences. A mechanical failure strands six of them in the wilderness. Their responses to that world and to their socialist biological heritage form much of the novel.[10] A measure of Aldiss' effectiveness is suggested by his recent comment that *Enemies of the System* and *Life in the West* have made him *persona non grata* in the Soviet Union, a situation he considers complimentary to him as writer.[11]

The novel traces the transformation of the "elite of the system" (Ch. 1) into "winners of the system" (Ch. 1), with its hints of reactionary capitalist competition; they are a "long way from the system," then aware of a "flaw in the system" (Ch. 7), and finally become "enemies of the system" (Ch. 11). *Homo uniformis* disintegrates, subtly but relentlessly. Characters are first isolated in a tourist bus, then isolated even more as the six go for help through the primitive terrain of Lysenka II.

56

Captured by mutants and caged, they never cease to believe—superficially, at least—in their status as the elite. They talk less about escape than philosophical fine-points of politics and polemics. They refuse to make independent decisions. One of them finally acts for himself and escapes, returning with a rescue party. For taking independent action, he is arrested as a subversive and a reactionary. In a final irony, the five who have proven their abilities to survive, who have acted throughout to return to the security of the utopian society they represent, are accused by the sixth of crimes against the state, including "deformed thought-processes," "misapplication of history," pessimism, and "intent to conspire with degenerate capitalists who scheme to take over control" of Lysenka II. In socialist jargon, as Aldiss imagines it a million years hence, the charges are applicable; in contemporary terms, however, the novel recounts disaster, preservation of human life, captivity and daring escape, and individual heroism—all anathema to *homo uniformis.*

As so often in Aldiss' writings, there is a close connection here between content and style, between physical setting and psychological exploration. The novel examines a classless utopian society celebrating the one-millionth anniversary of Biocom (biological communism), and much of the language parodies communist and socialist jargon. As a result, long passages seem little more than interminable polemics for socialist theory. The novel slows when it should quicken; for example, while being herded through passages in the primitives' caverns, the six do not try to escape but instead discuss how the existence of such primitives effects their political philosophy. When they do discuss escape, it is only in terms of political concensus, not individual action.

Such apparent flaws, however, are not only purposeful but necessary. The language *is* the novel. The stiffness and formality of the innumerable discussions reflect the basic flaw of *homo uniformis*—their inability to act independently. An earlier species, *homo sapiens,* was at the mercy of three physiological systems, the Central Nervous System, the Autonomic Nervous System, and the Neocortex—corresponding roughly to Tom, Barry, and the Other in *Brothers of the Head.* Unable to control or balance the three, humanity remained "divided against itself mentally and socially and politically and—well, in every way conceivable" (Ch. 2). The invention of the Bioshunt, however, allowed conscious control over all physiological processes, banishing emotional instability—including its manifestation as war, mental illness, religion, and romantic love. For a million years, the new humanity establishes itself through the galaxy; yet in the space of just over one hundred pages, Aldiss shows that there has been no essential change in the species. There is only a facade of progress, as in Malacia. Given the proper conditions, he argues, *homo sapiens* resurfaces, destroying the illusory unity prized by the new system.

To make this resurgence believable, Aldiss again uses landscapes as models for the psychological states he investigates. The six tourists represent the elite of the new system: the planet they visit is "primitive, regressive, and of an entirely lower politico-evolutionary order" (Ch. 10).

Among the native flora they see a "cage tree"; each tree, their guide explains, is a colony of up to fifteen individuals. The trunks grow from a common base, rejoining a dozen feet up to form a cage. It is, the guide contends (with a disregard for basic evolutionary principles that echoes an earlier Lysenko), "the first example of socialist unity to be found in the vegetable world on Lysenka" (Ch. 2). Later we see cages again—only this time human-constructed. The six tourists are isolated from each other and forced to independence. Ironically, the image first introduced as an emblem of unity becomes an instrument for ultimate disunity.

As usual, Aldiss also embeds puns and word-games into the novel, with subtle symbols adding to its complexity and enjoyment. There are fifty-two tourists in the original group, arriving to celebrate a one-millionth anniversary—the yearly cycle repeated almost beyond imagination. In spite of this, the old humanity lies close to the surface; it is, one character notes, a criminal offense in many places to be labeled *homo sapiens*. Acronyms recall the contemporary penchant for jargon, while defining Aldiss' attitudes toward socialist agencies. The Institute for Pre-Utopian Studies becomes IPUS, with its suggestion of sickness and decay (cf. DOUCH[E] in *Greybeard*).

This love of words and play defines the central theme of the novel—stasis and entropy. *Homo uniformis* has achieved unity. But connections between the socialist universe of *ES* and the universe of *MT* are clear. The new system, one of the characters argues, moved slowly, generation after generation, as the old world died. Logic supplanted emotion: irrationality was abolished, along with womb-birth, family, art, religion. Yet what has been the result? "Nothing. In a million years, we have in fact achieved less than *sapiens* achieved in a century or so. . . . all we've done is entrench ourselves in the System like woodlice in an old log" (Ch. 10). The condemnation is double-edged. The old system represented disunity and division, but division is necessary for survival. The new represents perfect utopian unity, but is incapable of change or adaptation. Like Malacian society, the system based on Biocom is slowly coming to a halt. It is "a utopia that carries within itself the seeds of its own destruction," Willis McNelly concludes:

> The tensions here are East versus West; civilization versus primitivism; individualism versus humanity. Aldiss has taken the Marxist challenge seriously, crafting a novel that is both provocative and extrapolative.[12]

He has also created a novel which carries us forward into the 1980s, where Aldiss' interests are even more clearly focused in *Life in the West* and Helliconia.

Notes

[1]Letter to Larry Ashmead, 23 January 1968. An expanded version of this discussion of *Brothers of the Head* was presented at the International Conference for

the Fantastic in the Arts, March 1985, in Beaumont, TX.

[2]Wingrove refers to it as "the most perfect of Aldiss' novellas" (Griffin and Wingrove, p. 211).

[3]While *Brothers of the Head* was still in the galley stages, Mathews wrote that readers might assume the new work to be a sequel to *Barefoot,* but that such an assumption would be inaccurate (p. 59).

[4]Griffin and Wingrove, p. 213.

[5]In light of the theological levels touched in Aldiss' novel, it is worth noting that both Aldiss and Miller portray worlds destroying themselves through technology beyond the control of morality.

[6]In a typically Aldissian paradox, however, inner also mirrors outer, leaving the reader with no clear "key" for interpreting the matrix of observations and assumptions, as in *RPA.*

[7]"Stanzas from the Grand Chartreuse," 11. 85–86.

[8]Griffin and Wingrove, p. 213.

[9]Letter to Michael R. Collings, 22 January 1985.

[10]"Brian W. Aldiss," in *Science Fiction Writers: Critical Studies of the Major Authors from the Early Nineteenth Century to the Present Day,* ed. E. F. Bleiler, p. 255.

[11]Cited in *Fantasy Newsletter,* 67 (May 1984), p. 24.

[12]McNelly, p. 255.

X
Decade the 1980s:
Moreau's Other Island

In a chronological reading of Aldiss' novels, *Moreau's Other Island* seems anomalous. Published in 1981, it bears little resemblance to *Malacia, Brothers of the Head, Enemies of the System,* or Helliconia. Instead, it relates in both content and style to *Frankenstein Unbound* and "The Saliva Tree," understandable affinities, since it was completed shortly after *Frankenstein Unbound* and represents Aldiss' attempt to deal with and re-create Wells' vision as he had recently done with Shelley's. A work of "homage-exegesis," to borrow Wingrove's phrasing, *MOI* is "Dedicated to the spirit of H. G. Wells: The Master" and shows the depth of Aldiss' interest in Wells' fictions while writing *BYS*. Wingrove states that

> Aldiss' exegesis of Wells' "excellently dark" novel . . . is once again a reinterpretation through a modern perspective: one that retains the original's strong allegory whilst adding a depth of characterization that it lacked.[1]

After completing the manuscript, however, Aldiss was not fully satisfied and withheld it for some years, until outside pressures caused him to publish it. The resulting novel is more problematical than *Frankenstein Unbound*. Here, for perhaps the first time, Aldiss seems almost to repeat himself, something unusual in his fictions. Instead of pushing forward, exploring deeper possibilities of style and content, he seems to stand still, creating a narrative narrower than *Frankenstein Unbound,* attempting more perhaps, but achieving less.

There are, of course, differences in conception and execution between the two novels. *Frankenstein Unbound* moves back in time; Bodenland is transported into a nineteenth-century past in which myth and history have coalesced around Mary Shelley, Frankenstein, and the monster. Using Shelley's original, he adds strength upon strength, sharing her powers and developing an insight that re-creates the complexity of Shelley's vision. Frankenstein and the monster (and Mary Shelley) become larger than life as they manifest in the life of Joe Bodenland, who represents Aldiss' own time and place.

In *MOI*, on the other hand, Aldiss moves forward in time, bringing Wells' creation through our society and beyond. As a result, he cannot simply manipulate Wells' characters as he had done so brilliantly with Shelley's. Instead, he brings forward the intellectual framework of Wells' narrative, embodying it in new characters. The narrator is Calvin Roberts, an Under Secretary of State during the global war of 1996. When his space shuttle is sabotaged, he lands on an island in the Pacific (an ironic name, considering the novel's obsession with warfare). He is rescued by a beast-like native; even before he discovers the name of the island, he refers to the "jackal sneer" and "boarish element" in his rescuer. Later, when he hears that the natives are remnants of Moreau's original experimental stock, Roberts seems unable to believe it. He is at once too perceptive and too dull, although in justice to Aldiss it must be noted that, throughout the novel, Roberts reveals himself as a fool, a coward, and a manipulator, a characterization consistent with Aldiss' uses of the island as distillation of the insanity and as the will to destruction in the macrocosm. That destruction, he argues, is the result of manipulation by other men, more powerful than Roberts, but equally insensitive and imperceptive.

Mortimer Dart is Aldiss' Moreau-figure. After the characterizations in *Frankenstein Unbound,* he seems disappointing, although in some senses he is a worthy successor to Wells' Moreau. He is isolated by his scientific curiosity, obsessed with knowledge for its own sake and at whatever cost, and suffering a love–hate relationship with his work and his island. But he is also less fully developed than Bodenland or Frankenstein, a cardboard figure upon which Aldiss paints whatever message he needs. Dart is morally and physically a monster, on his own admission as deformed as his creatures. He is literally larger than life during much of the narrative, using a metal robot-like structure to walk. As the Master, surrounded by his prosthetic apparatus, he is nearly three-meters tall, with metal arms and legs, and an imposing voice amplified by built-in microphone. The apparatus conceals deformity, however, just as eventually Roberts' title and position hide deformities in his character. Dart is a victim of thalilomide, a 1960s biological bomb that recalls the "Accident" of *Greybeard.* He has neither arms nor legs; his hands and feet are deformed; and he has a penile deformity imagistically at odds with his pretentions to creativity.

The mention of the drug connects the isolated island with the surrounding world. Dart is as much monster as the Beast People: at one time, he deliberately and proudly catalogues similarities between himself and the Seal People. He is the result of scientific misdirection, yet fails to attain to the stature of Frankenstein or the monster, perhaps because Aldiss is too consciously creating a parable for our time.[2] He seems manipulated for the sake of the message, just as Dart and Roberts in turn manipulate others. The result is that it is difficult to emphathize fully with Dart's tragedy or with the tragedy of the island. Dart is more petulant than noble, peevish and trivial rather than tragic. The other humans are equally diminished. Hans Maastricht, the foreman, is a drunkard; and when he begins to develop to full humanity, he drowns. His funeral sparks rebellion among the Beasts, accelerating the disintegration of the island's fragile society. Another human, de Silva, appears only infrequently and serves as window dressing—assistant to the mad scientist. Even the tempting female,

61

Heather, is a distortion. She is human and allies herself with Roberts after the rebellion of the Beast People but finally reveals that she is a creature more dangerous than any created in Dart's laboratories—she is a government agent assigned to protect Dart. In the world Aldiss portrays, there is no one to trust. Everyone is flawed, deformed physically or psychically; all are more Beast than Human.

In addition, the novel concentrates overwhelmingly on war. The plot begins when Robert's ship crashes and continues as he discovers that Dart's researches—what Dart fittingly calls the "Frankenstein process"— are war-efforts subsidized by the United States government. Roberts begins by seeing everything dichotomized as either good or evil, light or dark, *us* or *them*. Suddenly, such sharp demarcations blur, and Roberts decides that he must escape the island and report Dart's inhuman practices, shutting down the experiment externally. He declares war on Dart, exploiting the other humans, the utopian Seal People, and the Beast People to achieve his ends. He lies, steals, imposes his will upon others, even indirectly causes the death of the remaining human, Warren—all to prove his power as Under Secretary of State.

The irony is that he is the true Frankenstein. His arrival on the island begins the sequence of disintegration and death. Maastricht has been a drunkard for years; only after Roberts arrives does that drunkenness lead to death. And from that death stem all of the others. Roberts' guilt runs even deeper, however; he is more than merely an intruder disrupting a stable society. He has in fact created the island called Moreau. Dart's experiments are funded by and, in the person of Heather, protected by Roberts' Department of State: "In a flash of terror," he says, "I saw myself back in Washington, turning up the Moreau file, issuing my blanket condemnation, only to find my own rubber-stamp signature on the original authorization" (Ch. 11). This development, coupled with overt references to Frankenstein and to the philosophy Aldiss developed through Victor Frankenstein, argues that *MOI* owes more to *Frankenstein Unbound* than is usual in Aldiss' *ouevre*. He tries to make more forceful points already well developed in *Frankenstein Unbound* and, as a result, *MOI* seems thinner, more didactic than extrapolative or exploratory. Aldiss already knows the answers this time, and the novel suffers because of that.

There is also a diffuseness about Aldiss' purposes here that seems unusual. He touches on a number of issues: the insanity of warfare; drug use and abuse; scientific research leading to unforeseen change. The novel tries to allow each point equal space, with the result that none develops as it should. The most critically flawed is the anti-war sentiment. *MOI* is an essay in conflict—human against human, human against animal, animal against animal, humanity against nature itself. Dolphins become deadly weapons implanted with nuclear charges and sent unknowingly on death missions. Dart's ultimate creations are the SRSR, "Standby Replacement Subrace," modified stock designed to survive the radiation humanity is about to release. Like Aldiss' *homo uniformis* in genesis and purpose, the SRSR are small humanoids whose skin inhibits radiation, whose increased metabolism enables them to reproduce rapidly and supply any surviving humans with a workforce to rebuild the world. They are, Dart boasts, perfect responses to the "sort of catastrophe scenario they are designed for" (Ch. 12). Humanity has given up hope and acknowledged that it cannot survive in its own world and that it is about to pull that world down. In terms of island society, Heather represents this view; her intellect and her instinct are openly at war, with little chance of reconciliation (Ch. 10). What Aldiss would later develop through a powerful symbol in *Brothers of the Head,* here he states rather too overtly in the chapter, "After the Fall." Significantly, in the opening lines of that chapter, Heather inadvertently defines Roberts' character by misnaming him "Calvin."

Thus religion is brought into the narrative, but in a curiously unfocused way. "After the Fall" is ambiguous, although clearly theological in its implications. Roberts "falls." He jumps from a pinnacle on the main island in an ironic inversion of Christ's temptation on the Pinnacle of the Temple, as Aldiss provides a counterbalance to Milton's *Paradise Lost* and *Paradise Regained.* Rescued by the Seal People, Roberts enters a Paradise of peace, security, escape from the insanity of Moreau Island, and, most important for him, total sexual freedom with the Seal-woman Lorta and a five-year-old Japanese girl Satsu. The episode blends the paradisical and the lascivious, an oddity not even Roberts can explain. Elsewhere, Aldiss points to additional religious layerings. Roberts' first name, "Calvert," is several times confused with "Calvin" and "Calvary." One of the Beast People is crucified near the entrance to Dart's compound and stands a grisly watch over the gates; Aldiss points this out several times as the novel approaches its climax. Characters engage in long discussions of God, with Roberts as a vocal if hypocritical moralist and nominal Christian. And, of course, the question of Dart's manipulation of the Beast People and his own drug-caused deformity raise questions of free will and control. Yet these elements fail to coalesce, and seem finally more surface than essence.

This is not to argue that *MOI* fails as a novel, however. It is interesting and powerful, its weaknesses apparent primarily when compared with the strengths of *Frankenstein Unbound.* Viewed by itself, it shows a number of strengths.

One of the most interesting points develops subtly and is largely obscured in the American edition, re-titled *An Island Called Moreau.* As with *Non-Stop/Starship,* the change in title damages the novel. The American title points to an early passage describing Roberts as he drifts beneath the cliffs of the island, fearing that if he fails to land he will be carried out to sea and die. He notes a remarkable detail, a gigantic letter *M* carved into the cliff face. The letter seems "independent of meaning, to exist only for itself. Its very shape suggested a sturdy bipedal independence" (Ch. 1). The "Island Called Moreau" thus connects the themes of independence and isolation, meaninglessness, and human existence. The American title points primarily to *this* island.

The original title, however, suggests a different emphasis. "Moreau's Other Island" at first applies only to the island. It is named for Moreau, to be sure, but it is also another island on which a modern Moreau continues the work of his predecessor. Later, however, we discover a second "other island," one about which Aldiss seems more concerned. The physical island is a place of terror, pain, and inhumanity. But there *is* something worse. Throughout, Aldiss presents the island as microcosm. Many episodes, particularly those outlining the accelerating state of war on the island, parallel Roberts' descriptions of the outside world. And toward the end of the novel, Roberts discovers another "Moreau Island," which, while not physically present, is equally real and threatening. That island exists only in the dossiers in his office in Washington; it is a "doppelganger of the real island, a tidy little utopia" made of words on pages. It is an abstraction, where everything balances with an accountant's precision. All that it lacks is humanity. *That* island, Roberts decides, must be destroyed, that archetype for technological meddling, for experiments diminishing the nature of humanity itself (Ch. 11). There are clearly ironic parallels between the two islands. The "neat figures" oppose the bestial figures Roberts first sees; the careful balancing underscores the imbalance Roberts introduces. But the essential point is quite simply that Moreau Island is not ultimately the site of inhumane experimentation with the plasticity of flesh and the malleability of life. It only manifests a blind bureaucracy that passes for civilization in the twentieth century. The island is only a symptom; the disease lies elsewhere, in the body to which the island is tenuously connected—the "outside world." And that world, like Moreau Island, seems determined to destroy itself.

This is the final message of the novel. The Prologue and Epilogue are written in objective, third-person prose, opposing Roberts' first-person narrative. After the formality of the Prologue, which introduces the "contrast between land and sea, conscious and unconscious [that is] Aldiss' modern extrapolation of Wells' tale of the animal-in-man and the man-in-animal,"[3] we quickly learn not to trust Roberts. He is too self-absorbed, too much of the world Aldiss criticizes. He instructs through example rather than precept, like Bodenland in *Frankenstein Unbound*. But here, Aldiss brackets the narrative in an objective frame, with an unnamed and unnameable narrator whom we *can* trust. Through the voice of this observer, the novel ends with a warning. Earth and sea represent the conscious and the unconscious, reason and instinct, and "until humanity comes to an armistice between these yin-yang factors, there is no armistice possible on Earth. The bombs will fall" ("Epilogue"), again reminiscent of the conclusion of Walter M. Miller, Jr.'s *A Canticle for Leibowitz*. Leading nicely into the central symbol of Helliconia, the point is both valid and critical; but *Brothers of the Head* makes it more powerfully and less dogmatically, while the Helliconia volumes subsume didacticism beneath a stronger narrative structure and a far more involved imaginary world. In spite of the concluding tone, however, *MOI* does attain to a certain strength. It is the work of a master, and even through its weaknesses it remains worth reading. If it suffers, it is through the power of the novels surrounding it.

Notes

[1] Griffin and Wingrove, p. 170.

[2] Griffin and Wingrove, p. 170. Wingrove points to Aldiss' manipulation of symbol in the Prologue and Epilogue as enhancing the allegorical sense of the novel.

[3] Griffin and Wingrove, p. 170.

XI
Decade the 1980s:
Life in the West, Helliconia Spring, Helliconia Summer, and *Helliconia Winter*

In January 1982, Aldiss wrote,

> I regard *Helliconia* as a three-volume novel rather than a trilogy; the parts will fit snugly together to form a unity and a resolution greater than one expects from a trilogy.[1]

Atheneum's publicity sheet quotes Aldiss' comment that the series would be "the climax of my career."[2] Almost three years later, in September 1984, Aldiss discussed links between Helliconia and his earlier works,

> . . . in particular *Non-Stop* and *Hothouse*, not to mention *Galaxies Like Grains of Sand.* . . . There, the division between man and nature was not properly resolved: now it is faced and accepted in all its implications. In Tom Clareson's interesting review of *Summer* in *Extrapolation*, he feared a final plunge into Arnoldian gloom. I believe I have gone beyond all that, even though I subsume the new sinister meaning to "winter" coined since I embarked on the project.[3]

In many ways, *Helliconia* represents a culmination in Aldiss' career. All three volumes are implicit in *Non-Stop*, published almost three decades before, as if he has finally completed investigating change, to the extent that it may be completed. The Helliconia volumes summarize themes, characters, and narrative strategies, drawing on virtually everything Aldiss has written. The conclusion of *Helliconia Winter*, for example, echoes the final chapter of *Frankenstein Unbound* as protagonists find themselves in a world of darkness and snow, waiting for . . . something. Billy Xiao Pin's intrusion parallels Roberts' in *MOI*. The human stupidity and cruelty revealed in *Greybeard* also find a place in Helliconia when, for instance, the Oligarch in *Winter* destroys the Phagors, which carry the virus causing the Fat Death and the Bone Fever, without which humans on Helliconia could not survive. Like the scientists in *Greybeard*, Helliconia's rulers seem intent on limiting their own survival as a species; *Winter* touches upon similar themes from *The Dark Light Years* and *Earthworks*. The sense of Renaissance culture, of change within stasis, suggests *The Malacia Tapestry*. And Aldiss' tripartite examination of human psychology in *Brothers of the Head* echoes throughout Helliconia—Earth, Helliconia, and Avernus suggest a similar division.

To consider Helliconia as *a* culmination (certainly not *the* culmination) seems just. It is Aldiss' most ambitious undertaking to date; and in the complex connections between Helliconia and Earth, between the Helliconia volumes and everything Aldiss has previously achieved, Helliconia establishes its importance in Aldiss' canon.

In the review of *Helliconia Spring* Aldiss alluded to, Clareson cites a prefatory note "referring to a supposed previous book, *Life in the West*" and defining Helliconia as a metaphor for the contemporary world.[4] *Life in the West* is critical to understanding Helliconia, even though it is difficult for American readers to locate; Clareson is not the only critic to imply that it might even be fictitious, part of the narrative strategy of Helliconia. Yet *LW* is worth the effort to find (and Aldiss has indicated some interest from American publishers in reprinting it), not the least because it presages Helliconia in structure and purpose. *LW* is mainstream fiction, but frequently discusses science fiction: "Despite the popular misconception that it's all about space," one character says about the genre, "it's actually more important than that. It's all about everything" (Ch. 10).

Structurally, *LW* expands Aldiss' narrative strategy of fragmenting and re-integrating time. Chronology serves plot as Aldiss balances the private life of Thomas Squire with his public life and the implications of an East/West confrontation. Squire produces a television series entitled *Frankenstein Among the Arts*, itself suggestive in light of Aldiss' conclusions in *Frankenstein Unbound*. Squire is also a retired spy-assassin who once worked in Yugoslavia, another connection with Aldiss, whose visits to that country resulted in his *Cities and Stones: A Traveller's Guide to Yugoslavia* (1966). Squire's past makes problematical his relationship with a possible Russian defector attending the First International Congress of Intergraphic Criticism. As Aldiss weaves chapters from each of the narrative strands into a complex of disrupted time, he parallels Squire's sense of personal and public disintegration with that of Western society as a whole. The role of culture and the arts in contemporary society; contradictions between public and private, new and old, East and West, art and life, stasis and change; time and its relation to culture—all appear in *LW*, handled with Aldiss' typical wit and ingenuity. The novel introduces Helliconia, to be sure, but it also defines issues Aldiss has explored for decades; as Thomas Squire says in a different context, it "tells truth in showing how change is everywhere" (Ch. 10). Squire's own attempts to resist change—and his final acceptance of it—create the texture of *Life in the West*. By following Squire's conflicts, both internal and external, the reader understands more deeply what Aldiss sees as the "malaise sweeping the world" (*HSpr*, Prefatory letter). And by observing Aldiss as he anatomizes science fiction—referring to his own stories and novels, to his experiences in Malaysia and Singapore (which resulted in a recent short-story collection, *Foreign Bodies* [1981])—the reader steps outside the world of Thomas Squire to view his own world more objectively. In the final paragraph of *LW*, Squire meets his wife in a restaurant: "He knew . . . that Theresa—and Diedre, and he, and everything of which they were a part—were changed. Things would never be as they had been; that must be accepted (Ch. 14).

Coming as it does after the stasis of Malacia and the cataclysmic change in *Pile*, *LW* sets the tone for Helliconia.[5] Instead of Arnoldian gloom, we find mature acceptance. Things change. To pretend otherwise is not only foolish but disastrous. Like Thomas Squire, the Helliconians must accommodate to the cycle of seasons that defines their world, just as the humans on Earth must accommodate their own change, which in the final volume of Helliconia results not in pessimism but in an empathic connection among themselves and with sentience elsewhere in the universe. By the final chapter of *Helliconia Winter*, Earth/Gaia has become almost a character, a mother-figure inviting her children to exist within the framework of inevitable change.

The quest of virtually every one of Aldiss' major characters—for self, for understanding, for maturity—concludes in Helliconia, as Lutherin shouts defiance into the icy wind that signals the onslaught of another Great Winter. Change happens; he adapts to it, relishes it, challenges it. Aldiss concludes *Winter* as he began *Spring*, by quoting Lucretius: "The Earth passes through successive phases, so that it can no longer bear what it could, and it can now what it could not before." The Thomas Squire we see at the beginning of *LW* is not the same as appears in the final chapter; the Helliconia we see at the conclusion of *Winter* is not that which existed in the opening chapters of *Spring*. Nor is the Earth the same. Too much has happened; too much has changed. Yet the change itself is neither good nor bad. It merely is.

Besides *LW*, other novels illuminate Aldiss' purposes in Helliconia, preeminently Anna Kavan's *Ice*.[6] Kavan influenced Aldiss greatly during the years before her death, so much so that in *Last Orders* (1977), which Aldiss considers among his most important short-story collections, he incorporates her as a character in several stories. More germane to Helliconia, however, in his introduction to the American edition of *Ice*, Aldiss wrote that

> The transitory was very much her [Kavan's] province. Perhaps the precarious stability of her life was best maintained by stressing the ever-shifting nature of human affairs. If so, *Ice* is certainly her finest achievement: the glaciers closing in—themselves things incapable of real permanence—mark the destruction of everything, from nationality to personality.[7]

This posthumous tribute to Kavan suggests Aldiss' own preoccupations in Helliconia, including the central image of encroaching ice so critical in *Winter* and present by inversion in *Spring*. In *Helliconia*, as in *Ice*, characters "do not leap up and embrace their catastrophe; nor do they flee from it; they accept it as part of life."[8] Even more to the point is Aldiss' summary of *Ice*:

68

. . . these troubled and nameless people move in a world of shifting catastrophe, through an anonymous Scandinavian-type country ("once prominent states had simply dropped out of existence"), against a background of meaningless and unceasing military activity.[9]

In large measure, this statement defines Helliconia, particularly *Winter*, as characters accept the oncoming Great Winter and re-define loyalties, priorities, and their essential natures to prepare for inevitable change. Everything—political ties, personal ties, religious ties—fades in significance when confronted with the single fact of winter.

Kavan's text provides multiple icons for understanding Helliconia. Her hero, searching for a woman lost in the midst of cataclysm, sees a girl standing on a boat. Other travelers crushed forward to watch the landing while she

. . . was left isolated . . . I could not detach my attention from her, kept on watching. What most struck me was her complete stillness. Such a passive attitude, suggesting both resistance and resignation, did not seem entirely normal in a young girl. She could not have been more motionless if she had been tied to the rail, and I thought how easily bonds could be hidden by the voluminous coat (Ch. 2).[10]

The image of both resistance and acceptance, of hidden bonds pressuring characters into virtual stasis until they understand the nature of change within their worlds, recurs throughout Helliconia, from Yuli's experiences in the caverns of Pannoval in *Spring* to Luterin's in the Great Wheel of Kharnabhar in *Winter*. Defiance coupled with acceptance, leading to understanding and survival defines the central movement in Helliconia and, in a sense, in all of Aldiss' fictions.

In addition to Kavan's anatomy of change, Aldiss' own studies of stasis enrich Helliconia. The static tapestry of Malacia balances the constantly shifting landscapes of Helliconia as the ice recedes in *Spring*, replaced by deserts so hot that forests burst into flame spontaneously in *Summer*, and finally by returning ice in *Winter*. A revolutionary named Naab in fact accuses Pannoval of the same disregard for change that characterized Malacia: "Generation by generation, you sink into inaction, your numbers grow less, Pannoval dies." *Pile: Petals from St Klaed's Computer* (1976) also defines this key issue in Helliconia in its discussion of resistance to change in a city very like Malacia, and the devastating results when Lord Scart introduces change into that structure.

Spring also harkens back to *Non-Stop*, as Shay Tal explains that "some disaster happened in the past, the long past. So complete was it that no one now can tell you what it was or how it came about" ("Embruddock: Prologue"). The final scene in *Spring*, the burning town of Embruddock representing the destruction of one attempt at stability, has analogues in the final scene of *Non-Stop*, as the ship fragments. Aldiss'

69

description in *Spring* could again serve for both:

> The human figures clustering about two antlered figures represented between them three generations. They began to move across the landscape as it faded from view. They would survive, though everyone else perished, though the kzahhn triumphed, for that was what befell.
> Even in the flames consuming Embruddock, new configurations were being born. Behind the ancipital mask of Wutra, Shiva—god of destruction and regeneration—was furiously at work on Helliconia (Ch. 15).

The observer-being-observed structure of Helliconia echoes *Report on Probability A*, but here Aldiss provides not only raw data but the matrices to interpret that data. Early in *Spring*, Yuli falls during his escape from the cave-fortress of Pannoval. Peering through a fissure in the ledge he clings to, he sees what seems to be a blue stone; suddenly, it resolves into a lake "or possibly a sea, since he had a glimpse only of a fragment of a whole whose size he could not attempt to guess" ("Prelude: Yuli"). From this perspective, buildings seem but grains of sand. As the novel progresses, however, more layers of observers are added, including humans on Avernus recording every datum of Helliconia, and humans on Earth watching—and being entertained by—transmissions from Avernus. Only at the conclusion of *Winter*, however, do the characters become fully aware of each other, as Earth establishes an empathic link with Helliconia itself, merging observer and observed in a way impossible in *RPA*.

Brothers of the Head similarly echoes in Helliconia, not only imagistically, in the triple division of Helliconia, Earth, and Avernus, but thematically as well. If *Brothers* represented an internal landscape externalized, a psychological study of disunity, Helliconia reverses the process. The external landscape, the incessant sweep of change across Helliconia, becomes internalized as individuals move toward unity—not just political or social unity, although they frequently apply, but more critically toward unity with their world. They must understand the forces of change and adapt accordingly. The lines from Matthew Arnold's "Stanzas from the Grand Chartreuse" could serve as an effective epigram for *Brothers*—there is little hope for a new world from the ruins of the old; in Helliconia, Aldiss is more concerned with transition between worlds. As he says at the end of the "Prelude" in *Spring*: "A new world was already poised to be born."

As interwoven as the Helliconia volumes are with Aldiss' earlier works, however, they are not merely Aldiss repeating himself. In Helliconia, Aldiss moves beyond what he has achieved. He creates a solar system more compatible with "hard SF" than is usual in Aldiss. His complex of binary stars, elliptical orbits, and wildly varying climatic conditions is carefully detailed and defined, certainly the most complicated science-fictional alternate world he has yet attempted. The planets in *Bow Down to Nul*, *The Dark Light Years*, or *Enemies of the System*, for example, were primarily single worlds; Aldiss was not interested in their physics. Nor was he concerned with the star system containing Malacia, which seems basically a manifestation of an alternate Earth. But in Helliconia, the physics are critical. In a sense, the novel is constructed on the skeleton of Aldiss' stellar system, with its precisely computed orbits and eclipses, its apastron and periastron for the planet Helliconia as it circles the star Batalix, which in turn orbits a second star, Freyr, in a Great Year lasting 2,592 Earth-years, with correspondingly elongated winters and summers. This planetary system resembles one Aldiss examined some years earlier in *Farewell, Fantastic Venus,* when he cited Richard Proctor's discussion of a theoretical inclination of Venus' axis:

> An inhabitant of the regions near either pole has to endure extremes of heat and cold, such as would suffice to destroy nearly every race of living beings subsisting upon the earth. . . . Certainly none of the human races upon our earth could bear the alterations between these more than polar terrors and an intensity of summer heat far exceeding any with which we are familiar on earth.[11]

As we might expect, however, Aldiss does not rely on the inherent interest of his planetary system to engage his readers, as do such writers as Robert Forward in *Dragon's Egg* or Hal Clement in *Mission of Gravity*.[12] Instead, Aldiss uses science to frame the most exciting element in Helliconia, the relationship of that system with our own world.

In *Spring,* Aldiss tantalizes. He introduces Avernus station and through it, Earth, but infrequently. Those few references (in italics, another device reminiscent of *RPA*) promise a deeper involvement with Earth, suggesting that the spectacle of Helliconia moving into spring may be in some senses peripheral to Aldiss' ultimate concerns.

In *Summer,* observers from Avernus enter into the action on Helliconia, as Billy Xiao Pin leaves Avernus for Helliconia . . . and death, since the helico virus that enables Helliconians to survive summer and winter invariably kills Earth-humans; Helliconia remains isolated from Earth. Avernus is, in turn, isolated from both—from Earth by three-thousand light years, from Helliconia by the surety of death.

Billy's presence alters that balance, however briefly. The italicized passages dealing with Avernus cease to be merely cold observations. Avernus is as critically sensitive to change as Helliconia itself—to the despair of separation from all other humans, to the tensions of centuries within an artificial world (again, a connection with *Non-Stop*), and to the sheer tedium of constantly observing and never participating . . . in a word, to stasis. When Billy touches Helliconia, the relationship between observer and observed blurs.

In *Winter,* Aldiss increasingly moves his focus from Helliconia to Earth. The narrative still concentrates on Helliconia, of course, but includes longer and longer italicized passages, until Earth and Helliconia are not isolated but parallel each other. Helliconia faces the cyclical threat of winter and summer—only in spring and fall is the planet truly habitable. Earth, in the meantime, has undergone a "Great Year" of its own. Nuclear warfare has isolated it even from its own children on Avernus; ironically, as Earth ceases transmitting to Avernus, and as the transmissions from Avernus play to emptiness on a devastated Earth, the inhabitants of Avernus themselves change, losing contact with their past and their purpose. They turn science to perversion, creating "perambulant pudendolls," enormous motile genitalia that symbolize the distortion and (more importantly), the boredom that destroys Avernus. Aldiss systematically aligns the three worlds; in spite of technological breakdowns, they are connected through the empathic powers developed by Earth humans adapting to an altered environment. Gaia, the Earth Mother, can touch the Original Beholder, the god-image of Helliconia. Observers become participants, losing some of their individuality to gain contact with other sentient species.

To make connections between Earth and Helliconia even more explicit, Aldiss uses a number of techniques. Most immediately, at the level of plot, Aldiss re-creates the history of Western civilization. At the core of Helliconia lies the question of order and stability within change. In "Prelude," Pannoval has achieved stability, but at the price of a stultifying priestly bureaucracy; the remainder of *Spring* traces an alternative movement in Embruddock. Beginning at the level of mere survival, the people progress through identifiable stages paralleling the development of Western culture on Earth. From survival, they move to rudimentary attempts at controlling nature through magic and ritual sacrifice, attaining finally to the beginnings of scientific investigation, inventing the telescope and charting eclipses. With increased knowledge they expand westward, across the river, to new lands beyond the waters, only to confront a new threat, the invading hordes of phagors led by the Kzahhn Hrr-Brahl Yprt. The first volume concludes with Embruddock in flames; for the moment, the momentum of civilization halts.

In *Summer,* Aldiss narrows from generations to weeks, delineating a society reminiscent of Renaissance Europe. Kings and generals war for supremacy, manipulating and manipulated by social forces, religious prejudice, and the developing impact of science. A rising entrepreneurial middle class at times almost eclipses the royal machinations of Jandol-Anganol or his deposed and imprisoned father VarpalAnganol. Court scenes, both religious and secular, describe the Holy Pannovalan Empire of the Father Supreme of the Church of Akhanaba, the Great C'Sarr Kilander IX—a reflection of Rensissance Catholicism blended with the Holy Roman Empire. By depicting battles that resolve nothing, societies increasingly aware of science and technology, and court intrigues both public and private, Aldiss creates a sumptuous world that is simultaneously imaginative creation and astute exegesis of history. The historicity is compounded by the expansiveness of the volume, which moves across the landscape of Helliconia from the distant reaches of northern Sibornal (perhaps a conflation of "Siberia" and "Hyperborea," suggesting northern extremes in human history and myth) to southern Hespagorat. As did *Spring, Summer* ends with fire—and with unresolved questions, focusing on the relationship between humans and phagors.

The third volume concludes this recapitulation of Western history, extrapolating into our possible future as Helliconia retrenches and stagnates. Political leaders, epitomized by the Oligarch, turn their backs on progress in vain attempts to preserve a *status quo* threatened by encroaching winter. The achievements of *Spring* and *Summer* have become obsolete; all that is possible is for individuals, such as Luterin, to accept the need to adapt. Much of *Winter* inverts the narrative movement of *Spring* as the Great Year draws to a close; instead of fire, ice threatens in the last chapter. Instead of cities or nations, individuals approach center stage as society dissolves under the weight of winter. Instead of moving into light and warmth, characters retreat into darkness and cold, symbolized best by the unceasing circle of the Great Wheel of Kharnabhar. In addition, by this time Earth has also undergone its own variant on "winter"— a nuclear winter as devastating and fragmenting as Helliconia's climatic one. The two worlds merge, finding final resolution in the image of Luterin, exhilarated, shaking his fist and yelling his defiance while "The wind took the sound and smothered it in the weight of falling snow."

Language also connects Helliconia to our world. In a review of *Spring,* David N. Samuelson refers to "the relentlessly flat style of the narrative. Sentences are more sturdy than graceful, wit at the verbal level conspicuously absent."[13] To an extent, this evaluation rings true. Aldiss deals as much with elemental forces as with individuals; in *Spring* particularly, his vision is so broad that characters become virtually abstractions. In speaking of the helico virus which so dramatically alters the history of Helliconia, for example, Aldiss says, "The disease stream of the virus, like an irresistible flood, affected the history of all through whose lands it swept its ways. Yet an individual virus, like a single drop of water, was negligible" (Ch. 13). In spite of the tighter focus of *Summer* and *Winter,* all three volumes continue this emphasis, as characters appear and disappear, momentarily embodying stereotypes or abstract principles. Their ultimate importance supersedes their individuality. One pivotal character in *Spring,* the phagor Kzahhn Hrr-Tryhk Hrast, appears on only two pages in the novel: he is captured during an attack on Embruddock and executed. His great-grandson Hrr-Brahl Yprt initiates the crusade against humans that finally destroys Embruddock itself. And one of the most important "characters" in the novel never actually appears—the helico virus, visible only through its effects on civilizations.

As a result, the narrative may seem flat. But wit and humor are certainly not absent. Aldiss' love of verbal permutation pervades Helliconia. Names occasionally suggest a Swiftian humor—the Borlien priest in *Spring,* Father Bondorlonganon, seems Brobdingnagian by name alone. Later, in

Summer, Aldiss suggests character traits by naming his beautiful and regal queen MyrdemIngalla, and her proud, ambitious husband JandolAnganol. And there are sentences in which Aldiss enjoys pure verbal play, as when he tells of Laintal Ay being nursed to health by a *snoktruix* (an ingenious combination of "Earthly" phonemes). "As far as he could ever understand the word," Aldiss explains, "snoktruix meant a kind of healer; also stealer, dealer, and, above all, feeler" (*Spring,* 14). Other nouns resemble English words, simultaneously forcing the reader to visualize Helliconia in terms of Earth and allowing for particularly precise descriptions: hoxneys, the chief beasts of burden in Embruddock, suggest both horse and oxen; the chief recreation cavern in Pannoval is named Reck; and the ghosts to which characters descend in pauk (a hypnotic state) and which often serve as confessors are called fessups or gossies, recalling the older meaning of *gossip.*

This verbal texture extends more deeply than mere surface detail, however. The chief enemies of humanity on Helliconia are the phagors. They are truly menacing and well named, evoking the Greek *phagos,* "eating." Phagors are anthropophagous, eaters of humans, often used as executioners by human rulers, biting out the throats of the condemned. Male phagors are "stalluns," the females "gillots" or "fillocks," words which echo *stallion, filly,* and *gill* ("girl") to suggest a relationship with Earth, as does the phagor's military title *Kzahhn,* a conflation of *Khan* and *Czar* which leads in return to "C'Sarr," another connection with terrestrial history.

Nowhere in Helliconia is language more multi-valued than in the names of the planet and its system. *Helliconia* immediately evokes classical mythology—Mount Helicon and the Heliconian springs. My original response to the title of the first volume, in fact, was that the novel would involve the sacred mountain of Muses, distanced from all human activity. Paradoxically, Heliconia is appropriate for Aldiss' world. The muses, after all, influenced art and culture. Initially, Helliconia knows little of either; in *Spring* Aldiss writes that, beyond story-telling, the people of Embruddock have lost virtually all forms of art. The three volumes detail the gradual rise and subsequent decline of culture as the planet moves through climatic cycles, a theme reminiscent of Asimov's "Nightfall," with its recurrent dissolution of society during periodic eclipses.[14]

The difference in spelling, however, allows for a number of additional possibilities. Dividing the word after the first syllable results in *hell-icon.* As it first appears in *Spring,* Helliconia is indeed hellish, an icon of darkness and despair. As in Dante's vision, we find both ice and fire, extremes of torture and destruction. Only in the interim, during spring and fall, does the Helliconian Great Year encourage life, yet those segments of the Year contain other threats—Bone Fever and Fat Death, each killing nearly half of the population in preparation for the next climatic change.

The suggestions of the planet as an icon of Hell are emphasized by

74

additional place names. A number of satellites orbit Helliconia. Three are natural and reaffirm the mythic connections with Western traditions: Ipocrene, Aganip, and Copaise—the first two named for springs on Mount Helicon marking the hoofprints of Pegasus, the third for a nearby lake. The fourth, however, is artificial. Known on Helliconia as Kaidaw, after the animal used as a mount by the phagors, but also called Avernus, it is a space-station inhabited by descendants of colonists who traveled the three-thousand light years from Earth. Its name is also appropriately the name of the lake opening into the underworld in Roman mythology—literally a mouth into Hell. The scientists on Avernus transmit images from Helliconia to Earth by way of a receiver on Pluto's moon Charon, completing the mythic pattern of hell and the underworld.

But Aldiss is not yet finished. Late in *Spring,* he comments that the planet's name originated in a Phagorian term, "HrI-Ichor-Yhar." *Ichor* again has classical antecedents, denoting the fluid in the veins of the gods. Aldiss frequently refers to the yellowish blood of the phagors as "ichor," doubly ironic when one of the key discoveries in *Spring* is that phagors once ruled Embruddock and were later worshipped as gods in the manifestation of Akha, god of darkness and the underworld. Again, the word itself seems to complete a complex of images circling back on themselves, beginning and ending with gods and the underworld.

In a splendid turn of image, Aldiss suggests yet another possibility in the name of the planet. Scientists in Avernus know of the deadly virus, which they refer to as the "helico virus." The word, appropriately a form of *Helliconia* without the doubled *L,* corresponds to *helix,* symbolizing the eternal intertwining of light and dark, heat and cold, life and death that is Helliconia. It manifests in the narrative as the ever-present "circle or wheel with a smaller circle at its center. From the center circle, two opposed curved spokes radiated to the outer one" (*Spring,* "Prelude: Yuli"). Aldiss continually returns to this image, using it to represent not only the cycles of winter and summer, but the orbits of Helliconia about Batalix and Batalix around Freyr, and the multiple dualities implicit throughout—diversity and unity, stasis and change, love and hatred, earth and sky, underworld and overworld, microcosm and macrocosm.

In addition, the books themselves represent a helical movement within Aldiss' career. In discussing his writing of the late 1970s and early 1980s, Aldiss wrote that after a

> . . . period of disorientation, and of intense inward struggle, a sense of integration and power descended. With that I was able to embark on Helliconia. Interestingly, the nucleus of the Helliconia idea—and the determination necessary—came suddenly, as I was writing a letter to a friend. Even the name 'Helliconia' . . . arrived almost without thought: it was the delightful mountain of the muses; it was also Hell; and heliconia is also the name of a fragile butterfly inhabiting the tropics.[15]

It is also, it might be noted in passing, the name of an exotic flower indiginous to tropical America. It is all of these, and more, elements twisting in on themselves and out again, each curve of the helix exposing other possibilities inherent in a text that fully demonstrates Aldiss' mastery over language, meaning, and verbal texture.

The three volumes of *Helliconia* are, by any estimation, extraordinary, ambitious enough to merit attention by themselves as they encompass nearly half of the Helliconian Great Year, from the beginnings of spring to the beginnings of winter, re-creating cultural changes implicit over hundreds of years. At one point, pausing to explain how Helliconia became part of such an intricate stellar system, Aldiss extends his narrative millions of years into the past, tracing the history of phagorian and human evolution. The setting is attractive, with the intricate ballet of planet and moons and stars and their relationship to our own system. Only an author such as Aldiss—who has immersed himself in questions of stasis and change, entropy, ecological balance, and underlying definitions of what it is to be human and who has consistently explored their possibilities for three decades—could have brought such a vision to life.

And, as one expects from Aldiss, he does so without succumbing to the temptation of the easy, dramatic, science-fiction/space-opera ending. The individual volumes are difficult. *Spring* requires that readers extend their perspectives to include generations, not individuals; to work through a ninety-page prelude introducing virtually every thematic, symbolic, and imagistic pattern in all three volumes, including Aldiss' extraordinary use of necrogenic life (animals born only through the deaths of their parents). On Helliconia, as on Earth, the new can survive only as the old accept change and die. *Summer* narrows the focus from generations to six weeks, yet further complicates the narrative by fragmenting time and re-structuring it, forcing readers to integrate the narrative. And at the end of *Winter*, Luterin's imprisonment in the Great Wheel of Kharnabhar (completing and reversing Yuli's imprisonment in Pannoval two volumes earlier); the final images of encroaching cold and stasis; the understanding that to have survived change is itself a feat of true heroism; the empathic connections between Helliconia and Earth that allow us to see ourselves indirectly and directly—all of these combine to create a reading experience not easily dismissed or forgotten. *Winter* clarifies the connections between Earth and Helliconia, both through parallels and through contrasts; it combines the breadth and scope of *Spring* with the fine detail of *Summer* and in doing so, provides a perfect step beyond what Aldiss achieved in *The Malacia Tapestry*. It satisfactorily concludes themes that have engaged Aldiss for years; as he wrote recently, "without intending it that way, this final volume will be a culmination of much that has gone before, rendering some implicit material much more explicit."[16]

There will be much more, we hope, beyond Helliconia; but the intricacy and complexity of this vision assure Aldiss of continuing attention. As he himself wrote in the conclusion to "Creatures of Apogee,"

All [is] hushed after the storm of Change, except the wail of
atmosphere with its new winds.
Then the creatures of perihelion . . . muster themselves, and
. . . begin to ascend the stairs.[17]

Helliconia is complete; there is a moment of rest as we await the new.

Notes

[1] Cited in *Science Fiction and Fantasy Book Review,* 5 (June 1982), p. 19.

[2] *SFFBR,* 5 (June 1982), p. 19; appended to reviews by David N. Samuelson
and Willis E. McNelly.

[3] Letter to Michael R. Collings, 26 September 1984.

[4] Thomas D. Clareson, "Star Cluster: Nebula Time Again," *Extrapolation,* 24,
No. 1 (Spring 1983), 89–90.

[5] See also my review of *LW* in *Fantasy Review,* 67 (May 1984), p. 24.

[6] In *Last Orders* (1977), which Aldiss considers as one of his most important
collections, he incorporates Kavan as a character in "Enigma 4: The Eternal Theme
of Exile" (pp. 139–146) and four other stories. In a letter to Michael R. Collings,
7 September 1983, Aldiss wrote that in the mid-seventies, "life became rather difficult and the volume which truly deals with these difficulties is *Last Orders."*

[7] "Introduction" to Anna Kavan's *Ice* (Garden City, NY: Doubleday, 1970),
p. v.

[8] "Introduction," p. ix.

[9] "Introduction," p. xii.

[10] For additional information on Kavan, see Janet Byrne, "Moving Toward
Entropy: Anna Kavan's Science Fiction Mentality," *Extrapolation,* 23, No. 1 (Spring
1982), pp. 5-11; Aldiss' *BYS* (New York: Schocken, 1974), 316–317; and his "In
Memoriam: Anna Kavan," in *Nebula Award Stories 4,* ed. Poul Anderson (New York:
Doubleday, 1969).

[11] *All About Venus* (New York: Dell, 1968), 209: citing Richard Proctor, *Other
Worlds Than Ours* (1870). Aldiss notes that Proctor's theories proved to be overstated, but the distance from Proctor's conclusions to Helliconia seems not that great.

[12] Hal Clement, *Mission of Gravity* (Garden City, NY: Doubleday, 1954);
Robert L. Forward, *Dragon's Egg* (New York: Ballantine, 1980). In discussing his
novel at the Eaton Conference on Science Fiction (University of California, River-
side, 1983), Dr. Forward indicated that his novel was based heavily on science,
virtually everything a logical outgrowth of the physics of a neutron star.

[13] *Science Fiction and Fantasy Book Review,* 5 (June 1982), p. 18.

[14] In *Nightfall and Other Stories* (Garden City, NY: Doubleday, 1969).

[15] Letter to Michael R. Collings, 7 September 1983.

[16] Letter to Michael R. Collings, 14 December 1983.

[17] In *Last Orders and Other Stories* (London: Triad Panther, 1979), p. 27. Rpt.
of original edition, London: Jonathan Cape, 1977.

XII
The Short Fiction

While much of Aldiss' energy has been directed toward novels, he has also published over three-hundred short stories, making him one of the most prolific authors in the field. While many of his short stories are inaccessible to most readers (for example, a number appeared in the British *New Worlds SF,* which is quite difficult to find), Aldiss published others as parts of collections. Beginning with *Space, Time and Nathaniel* in 1957, Aldiss has published *No Time Like Tomorrow* (1959), *The Canopy of Time* (1959), *Galaxies Like Grains of Sand* (1960), *Equator* (1961), *The Airs of Earth* (1963), *Starswarm* (1964), *Best Science Fiction Stories of Brian W. Aldiss* (1966; reprinted as *But Who Can Replace a Man?*), *The Saliva Tree and Other Strange Growths* (1966), *Intangibles, Inc., and Other Stories* (1969), *A Brian Aldiss Omnibus* (1969), *Neanderthal Planet* (1970), *The Moment of Eclipse* (1970), *The Book of Brian Aldiss* (1972; reprinted as *The Comic Inferno*), *Last Orders and Other Stories* (1977), *New Arrivals, Old Encounters* (1980), *Foreign Bodies* (1981), *Best of Aldiss* (1983; a British magazine collection), and *Seasons in Flight* (1984).

While the sheer number of volumes attests to his productivity, it does not indicate the care with which the individual collections were assembled; in many instances, they approach the coherence and unity of novels, while several of his novels—including *Hothouse, Barefoot, Report,* and parts of *Malacia*—appeared first as short stories. Clearly, the dividing line between the two genres is unusually fluid for Aldiss.

In a study as limited as this, it is impossible to examine the short fiction as carefully as it deserves. But from his earliest stories, the hallmarks of his imigination, humor, and deep concern for humanity are present. In his first collection, *STAN,* for example, we already see much that Aldiss will refine during the next decades. *STAN* is impressive, even after almost thirty years and over two-hundred more stories. It defines its themes in its title and in the arrangement of the Table of Contents: four stories under the heading "Space"; four under "Time"; and six under "Nathaniel and Other People." In the stories, Aldiss examines the relationship of space and time and their impact upon humanity. To return to the initial metaphor of Aldiss as map-maker, *STAN* begins surveying the landscape that Aldiss would explore throughout his career.

The first story, "T," demonstrates the control that marks Aldiss as a writer. It is a curious tale, shorn of many elements one expects in a science-fiction story from the late 1950s. There is essentially only one character, T, a biological construct sent to destroy the Earth. Aldiss distorts space and time as T moves backward through time to destroy Earth before it threatens the empire. A plot summary suggests stereotypic space opera, but that is precisely what the story does *not* deliver. Instead, Aldiss creates empathy for T, defining coldly and dispassionately the genetic and biological engineering that created the lump of barely sentient and barely animate tissue, without thought or loneliness or self-awareness, whose only function is to watch a thin red/green line moving through the space-time continuum. His fellows are destroyed through a number of accidents, until only three of the original twelve appear in the solar system, some two-hundred years later in T's time-frame but before the appearance of life on Earth.

T and his fellows fulfill their mission—to destroy the seventh planet, counting inward from the boundaries of the system. And then Aldiss springs his joke, pointing up the inherent absurdities of a tale based on time travel. The plan succeeds; the sixth planet is shattered accidentally, and the seventh destroyed. But they had read the map backward: "If they had read it aright, they would have seen. . . . " Sol originally had nine planets; Earth is the seventh *only after* the asteroid planet and T's planet have been destroyed. The future remains unchanged.

That Aldiss intended his collections as quasi-novels is quite clear in *Galaxies Like Grains of Sand.* Although all of the stories had earlier appeared in magazines, Aldiss organized them into a coherent unity, ignoring the chronology of publication and giving them additional titles to suggest the place of each in his narrative: "The War Millennia," "The Sterile Millennia," "The Robot Millennia," and so on, culminating in "The Megalopolis Millennia" and "The Ultimate Millennia." Between each section, he interpolates interchapters, bridging narrative gaps and swinging the reader's attention to the new tale. The collection begins with "a strange past world, where clouds of nationalism have gathered and broken into a storm of war. Over the forgotten continents—Asia, America, Africa—missiles of destruction fly" (Ch. 1). Aldiss systematically describes permutations in society and humanity over generations, each story focusing on a particular change, until, in "The Ultimate Millennia . . . Visiting Amoeba," Aldiss describes the dissolution of the galaxy itself. The story is powerful, imaginative and iconoclastic, from its initial second-person narrative stance to its final evocation of triumph and defeat. "Nothing is meant to last," Aldiss writes, echoing C. S. Lewis' Oyarsa and Sorns on Malacandra; even galaxies must die. Into the old galaxy something new has intruded, a character whose molecules are themselves new, powerful. He is "the one fresh factor in an exhausted galaxy" (Ch. 8, section 8). Through him, humanity, represented by the Highest, discovers the mortality of the galaxy . . . and the fact that the intrusion of new elements has hastened its death. "What should be told to the people of the Galaxy," the Highest asks.

"Tell them what a galaxy is. . . . Don't soften it. They are brave. Explain to them once more that there are galaxies like grains of sand, each galaxy a cosmic laboratory for the blind experiments of nature. Explain to them how little individual lives mean compared to the unknown goals of the race. Tell them—tell them that this laboratory is closing. A newer one, with more modern equipment, is opening just down the street."

"They shall be told," the Highest said, his face a shadow as night fell upon the old city and the stars (Ch. 8, section 8).

Of the collections, *Last Orders* is perhaps the most powerful and the most difficult. It is a complex of maps and mapmakers, from the map-like cracks on the roof in "Last Orders" to "cartographic excursions" in "The Immortality Crew," a non-story segment of "Enigma 2: Diagrams for Three Stories"; to Chin Ping Neverson's map and "homeopathic finches" that chart out the future in "Waiting for the Universe to Begin," part one of "Enigma 3: The Aperture Moment"; to "predestinographologists in "Live? Our Computers Will Do That For Us." Aldiss refers back to his earlier novels, to themes he has dealth with before, including art and life, time, stasis and change. In turn, subsequent novels borrow from *Last Orders:* "Creatures of Apogee" reads like a sketch for Helliconia.

Philip E. Smith's "*Last Orders* and First Principles for the Interpretation of Aldiss' Enigmas" argues that *Last Orders* presents a blueprint for Aldiss' theories of science fiction. Beginning with the "Author's Note," a narrative fragment initialled B. W. A., and the first story, "Last Orders," the collection "contains mutually referential, reflexive, self-aware fictions concerned with the interplay of reality and artifice; its structure and content suggest not only a method of reading and interpreting the text, but also a theory about science fiction."[1] Among other things, Smith points to the "Enigmas," which Aldiss describes as

> . . . slightly surreal escapades grouped in threesomes—a form which provides the chance for cross references and certain small alternatives not always available in one story. I've always admired fiction which avoids glib explanations and espouses the sheer inexplicability of the universe (hence an affection, I suppose, for Hardy, Dostoevsky, Kafka, and Kavan); these attempts are dedicated to the enigmatic universe in which we find ourselves.[2]

In *Last Orders,* the five sets of enigmas vary from completed narratives to sketches for possibilities to imagistic suggestions. In part, the difficulty of the collection (and its power) lies in its transferring part of the responsibility for interpretation onto the reader. Aldiss is willing to suggest—to provide maps—but the reader must follow those maps and determine precisely where they lead.

In the "Author's Note" Aldiss writes:

And the man in the sharp suit said, "People want to be cheered up. They want to hear about real things."

"One or the other you can have. Not both. See, my stories are about human woes, non-communication, disappointment, endurance, acceptance, love. Aren't those things real enough? Nobody's fool enough to imagine that any near-future developments will obliterate them. Change there will be . . . But the new old blues sing on forever . . ."

Everyone in the crowd was drinking fast, laughing and gesticulating. They knew the world was going to end next week.

That range of possibility, coupled with the imminence of a disaster frozen in time (what Aldiss elsewhere calls the "paralysis of time") forms *Last Orders*, as it formed so many of Aldiss' other fictions.

Following *LO*, Aldiss published several other collections. *Foreign Bodies* has the distinction of being perhaps the scarcest first edition of his works; published in Singapore by Chopmen in an edition of two hundred, it is more mainstream than science fiction. Two of the stories, however, touch upon the fantastic. "Boat Animals" is a fantastic/allegorical treatment of the plight of the Boat People in the Far East. Ironic and humorous, it becomes fiercely biting at times, in both its situations and in its fine details. "The Skeleton" is brief, enigmatic, yet ultimately convincing—within its simplicity is a strong sense of meaning, relating East with West. The longest piece, "Frontiers," is less strictly fantastic, defining instead the balance between East and West in contemporary Asia.

Aldiss' most recent collection, *Seasons in Flight* (1984), continues his explorations into landscapes and style. The ten tales include two older stories—"The O in Jose" (1966) and "A Romance of the Equator" (1979)—along with eight others originally published since 1982: "The Other Side of the Lake," "The Gods in Flight," "The Blue Background," "Igur and the Mountain," "Incident in a Far Country," "The Girl Who Sang," "The Plain, The Endless Plain," and "Consolations of Age." As in his other collections, the stories here merge to suggest at least the outlines of a completed fiction; they use varying landscapes to trace the themes of war, of conflict between cultural beliefs, of pasts and futures that impinge upon the present. "The Girl Who Sang," for example, examines these themes against the backdrop of Helliconia. "The Other Side of the Lake," on the other hand, seems clearly located somewhere on our world, in our time; but there is a curiously timeless quality about the narrative that makes identifying a specific setting unnecessary. "The Plain, the Endless Plain" uses the abstraction of myth as it details the development of the Tribe through countless generations, through an unnamed land in an unnamed time, yet it finally redounds upon us as The Tribe finally sees the goal they have struggled for since Generation One—the misty outline of mountains against the edge of the unending plain:

The Tribe landed again, abuzz with excitement.

And at that moment enormous lights lit the sky overhead, such as none had ever known. And there were huge roaring noises. The ground shook. And a dazzling brilliance such as they had never known shone down from above and extinguished them.

Aldiss allows the reader final interpretation, but the analogues with Western culture are clear. As always, *Seasons in Flight* both satisfies and stimulates; the stories are self-contained narratives while simultaneously part of a larger whole—the vision of Brian Aldiss.

In general, Aldiss' short fiction defies easy classification. Each individual story must be considered on its own ground. Some seem straightforward science-fictional adventure, "Tyrant's Territory" (1962) for example. Others press beyond the conventional boundaries of science fiction: "Where the Lines Converge" (1977) or "The Small Stones of Tu Fu" (1978). Some, like the award-winning "The Saliva Tree" (1966), reflect Aldiss' literary heritage; others, including "Total Environment" (1968) and "That Uncomfortable Pause Between Life and Art" (1969) indicate Aldiss' concern for society, for problems such as overcrowding, and for the purposes of art. Many deserve special attention: "The New Father Christmas" (1958), with its eerie evocation of the fate of dying humanity in a machine culture; "Tyrant's Territory" (1962), with its finely realized alien life-forms; "Full Sun," with its intriguingly science-fictional perspective on the werewolf traditions of horror-fantasy; or "Super-Toys Last All Summer Long," with its understated irony. But no matter which story he tells, Aldiss can be counted on to provide interesting excursions into possibilities, excursions which not only entertain but engage the reader's imagination and intellect.

Notes

[1] The paper was read at the International Conference on the Fantastic in the Arts, sponsored by Florida Atlantic University, March 1983. It is scheduled for publication in volume four of the conference proceedings.

[2] Citing Brian W. Aldiss, "Afterword" to "Diagram for Three Enigmatic Stories," in *Final Stages,* ed. Edward L. Ferman and Barry N. Malzberg (New York: Charterhouse, 1974; rpt. New York: Penguin, 1975), p. 90.

XIII
Brian W. Aldiss as Critic

On the basis of his fiction alone, Aldiss' status as a major science-fiction writer is solid. But his influence is not limited to fictions; he is also an astute critic of literature and society, with over one-hundred reviews, many critical articles, and several full-length volumes, including *The Shape of Further Things: Speculation on Change* (1970), *Hell's Cartographers* (1975), *This World and Nearer Ones: Essays Exploring the Familiar* (1981), and *The Pale Shadow of Science* (1985). In addition, there are his articles in the *Best SF* series, co-edited by Harry Harrison, several of which form the basis for Robert E. Colbert's article, "Unbinding Frankenstein: The Science Fiction Criticism of Brian W. Aldiss."[1] And finally, there is his *Billion Year Spree: The True History of the Genre* (1973), which he recently indicated he is interested in revising and updating.

Aldiss' involvement in criticism began quite early, leading to his position as Literary Editor for the Oxford *Mail* from 1957 until 1969; in 1964 he and Harry Harrison co-edited one of the first non-fiction science-fiction journals, *SF Horizons,* espousing the thesis that

> ... what sf must have before all its potentials can be realised is a wide and flourishing literature of intelligent criticism.
>
> Without a doubt, a good deal of this criticism will employ the scalpel rather than the laurel crown, simply because of the bad work that persists within the sf field.... It is a skilled surgeon's saw that should be applied to the body of sf literature, so that the same hand that cuts away the gangrenous matter will revitalize the healthy.[2]

SF Horizons, while short-lived, did not lack for stature. The first issue includes "The Establishment Must Die and Rot ... ," a discussion of science fiction among Aldiss, C. S. Lewis, and Kingsley Amis, plus critical articles and fiction by Aldiss and Harrison, James Blish, Robert Conquest, G. D. Doherty, and Aldiss again, under the pseudonym C. C. Shackleton. The second issue repeats several of these contributors, adding an interview with William Burroughs, articles on Italian and Japanese science fiction, and poetry by C. S. Lewis.

As truncated as its life might have been, the journal was an auspicious and ambitious beginning. Six years later, Aldiss published *The Shape of Further Things,* a memoir, consciously paying homage to Wells and focusing partially upon the moon landing, partially upon Aldiss' thoughts and experiences during the time he worked on the manuscript. In many ways, however, one of his most lasting critical contributions is *Billion Year Spree*, a personal history/criticism of the genre completed after Aldiss' exhausting work on *Report* and *Barefoot* in the late sixties. David Wingrove suggests that the financial success of Aldiss' Horatio Stubbs novels allowed him time and ease to research the volume[3]; even more critically, though, *BYS* allowed Aldiss to return to science fiction, restoring his enthusiasm for fiction and stimulating *Frankenstein Unbound, Moreau's Other Island,* and "The Saliva Tree," pastiches based on his researches into the writings of Mary Shelley and H. G. Wells.

Initially, Aldiss showed the greatest confidence in the project that was to culminate after almost ten years in *BYS*.[4] In a letter to Diane Cleaver at Doubleday, Aldiss wrote:

> ... do let me repeat my great excitement about this book, which I'm sure is going to be beautiful and rich and full. It will not just be a hack repeat of whatever other people have said about Science Fiction. While it will stick to the facts, it is also going to be *numinous,* and contain the atmosphere as well as the dry bones.[5]

Originally, the book was designed as a collaboration between Aldiss and Philip Strick, Aldiss writing the opening chapters. Strick the later ones. An early provisional outline for the book shows the directions Aldiss envisioned:

1. FOREWORD
2. THE SHAPE OF PAST THINGS: A new perspective on the history of science-fiction.
3. PILGRIM FATHERS: Considerations of the themes and influence of late 19th- and early 20th-century writers, including Verne, Wells, Stapledon, Lewis.
4. THE HORROR MERCHANTS: Studies of s-f's debts to the macabre, with particular comment on Poe, Bierce, Lovecraft, Bloch, Matheson.
5. THE LIGHT FANTASTIC: Analysis of the work of Ray Bradbury, with particular concentration on *Fahrenheit 451.*
6. THE WARS OF THE ROBOTS: Analysis of the work of Isaac Asimov, concentrating on *The Naked Sun.*
7. BLOOD TIDE: Analysis of the work of Theodore Sturgeon, concentrating on *More Than Human.*
8. THE HUNTERS OF THE SNARK: Analysis of the work of A. E. van Vogt.
9. THE ODDS ARE AGAINST US: Analysis of the work of Arthur C. Clarke, concentrating on *2001: A Space Odyssey.*
10. STRANGERS IN OUR TIME: Analysis of the work of Robert A. Heinlein, concentrating on *Stranger in a Strange Land.*
11. WORDS FROM OUR SPONSORS: Analysis of the work

of Pohl and Kornbluth.

12. THE BURNING MAN: Analysis of the work of Alfred Bester, concentrating on *Tiger, Tiger*.

13. PROFITS OF DISASTER: Studies of the cataclysm through such writers as Philip Wylie, John Wyndham, John Christopher, Anthony Burgess, Edmund Cooper, Keith Roberts, Pat Frank, Algis Budrys, M. P. Shiel, Van Greenaway.

14. IS THERE STILL LIFE ON EARTH?: Analysis of the work of J. G. Ballard, concentrating on *The Crystal World*.

15. PROBABILITIES AT HAND: Analysis of the work of Brian Aldiss.

16. ELECTRIC SHEEP: Analysis of the work of Philip K. Dick.

17. NO SUCH THING AS PROGRESS: Analysis of the work of Kurt Vonnegut, Jr., concentrating on *Slaughterhouse Five*.

18. THE WEIGHT LIFTERS: Studies of s-f 'blockbusters' such as *Dune* (Herbert), *Canticle for Leibowitz* (Miller), *Stand on Zanzibar* (Brunner).

19. NEW WORLDS: Survey of recent developments in s-f, with mention of Moorcock, Zelazny, Spinrad, Disch, Ellison, Delany, Goulart. Conclusions.[6]

In January of 1972, however, Aldiss received the news that Strick would not be able to complete his chapters. Aldiss offered to either discard the project or continue on his own; Doubleday agreed with the latter. From that point, what had begun as an exciting project (Aldiss' letters to Doubleday at the time reflect his whole-hearted involvement with the book) became plagued with difficulties. There was some question about altering Aldiss' title to *The Thinkers and the Dreamers*; Aldiss responded that *Billion Year Spree* was the title he had used for over ten years in connection with the project, and besides, it "is an Aldiss title, and it does express something of the fun that I hope people will find in it...."[7] Then there were his concerns about other histories being published at the time, including James Gunn's and the Panshin's. Finally, and most critically, there were difficulties with the editing, with page corrections, with a poorly handled excerpt in *Works in Progress*, with early unfavorable reviews.[8] Aldiss felt that the book represented an important contribution to science fiction and was increasingly frustrated with how it was being handled.

For these reasons, *BYS* is a very different book from the one Aldiss described so enthusiastically in 1972. We find more expansive chapters, including the first chapter on Mary Shelley, so glaringly absent from the preliminary outline. Poe and Wells receive a chapter for themselves, while the science fiction of the thirties, forties, and fifties is consolidated into chapter-long overviews. Summary and survey replace in-depth analysis of individual authors and novels. Yet *BYS* is hardly a disappointment; while the original plan might have resulted in a vastly different book, the completed book is Aldiss throughout, with his own responses to the novels and personalities that form his chosen genre. It bears the stamp of his wit, his research, his wide reading in science fiction and in mainstream fiction. The seminal chapters on Shelley and Wells, and his highly influential "Pilgrim Fathers: Lucian and All That," were widely reprinted, helping to form critical approaches to the genre.

Of equal importance, *BYS* modulates between Aldiss' own writings, resolving the sense of enervation he felt following *RPA* and *Barefoot,* while introducing subsequent novels; the final paragraph of *BYS* connects his past with his future, through the mediation (as so often) of Anna Kavan:

> As in our inner beings, there are only three persons in *Ice.* The pursued and the pursuer often change roles, becoming indistinguishable. In that respect, they remind us of Frankenstein and his monster, and remind us how Frankenstein and monster, and their many later progeny, come to us from the inner being, where life, art, and science all begin.[9]

Among the many histories and critiques of science fiction, *BYS* is distinguished by being highly readable, highly enjoyable, and highly informative. It is as uniquely Aldiss as any of his novels; the only difference is that here Aldiss speaks directly. He keeps his field carefully in focus, defining both what it is and what it is not, assessing strengths and weaknesses in the genre itself and in its most famous practitioners. He brings it into contact with mainstream society—"Much as I love sf," he notes in the "Introduction" to *BYS*, "the greater world beyond it has always meant at least as much." Throughout, he maintains balance between the two, between Inwardness and Outwardness, between his function as objective critic and his role as writer in helping to create the genre he is anatomizing, and, to quote from the "Introduction" again, in "mapping the possible futures of the past."

In 1975, Aldiss published *SF Art,* a volume dedicated to science-fictional cover art, with Aldiss providing an eight-page introduction and marginal comments. The same year also saw the publication of *Hell's Cartographers: Some Personal Histories of Science Fiction Writers,* co-edited with Harry Harrison. The volume included contributions from Alfred Bester, Damon Knight, Frederik Pohl, and Robert Silverberg, along with Aldiss and Harrison. Aldiss' chapter, "Magic and Bare Boards," combines personal history with critical perspectives, giving an overview of Aldiss' childhood, his career, and his approach to writing. It refers to his early ambitions to become a poet, which, while diverted, have never been completely denied—witness such works as *Pile* and *Farewell to a Child,* as well as his activity in the Science Fiction Poetry Association. And it touches upon Aldiss' contemporaries in the field, upon the nature of science fiction itself, and upon its relation to mainstream fiction. It is, in many ways, an ideal short introduction to Aldiss through his own words and his own perspectives.

This World and Nearer Ones: Essays Exploring the Familiar is less personal, more outwardly oriented than his earlier volumes. In it, Aldiss writes that "the first duty of a reviewer is to summarize, with as straight a face as possible, the volume before him."[10] That criterion is difficult to follow with *This World,* simply because of his wit and humor, his excitement, and the overriding sense of his presence throughout the book. The essays, spanning nearly a decade, were revised for the book and co-ordinated into six sections: Writing, Hoping, Living, Seeing, Rough Justice, and This World. In each, Aldiss correlates science fiction with the world around us, including essays on individual writers, on the differences between British and American science fiction, and on language. The core of the collection, however, is the section on "Seeing," a discussion of art, science, and science fiction—and of past, present, and future. "SF Art: Strangeness with Beauty" is one of the most valuable articles, largely because it confronts these central concerns directly. Throughout, Aldiss draws on his wide reading and experience, making connections unnoticed by others; and at the end, that is what makes *This World* impressive—the enduring presence of Aldiss speaking about his world.

As was the case with Aldiss' short fiction, his criticism literally defies narrow definition. To glance quickly at a handful of books does injustice to the remaining articles, reviews, notes, addresses, and other means by which Aldiss defines himself as writer and his genre as literature. He insists throughout that science fiction be treated as a literary genre, that its division from mainstream fiction is at times arbitrary and artificial. He demands care from writers and consideration from readers. His criticism, like his fiction, is never facile, never too easy. Yet underneath it, as under his fiction, moves a restless mind, casting about for new ideas, testing them, and faithfully reporting their merits.

Notes

[1] *Extrapolation,* 23, No. 4 (1982), 333-44.

[2] Aldiss and Harrison, "Statement of Policy," *SF Horizons,* Spring 1964, pp. 3-4.

[3] Griffin and Wingrove, 158.

[4] Letter to Diane Cleaver, 25 April 1972. Huntington Library, San Marino, CA.

[5] Letter to Diane Cleaver, n.d. Huntington Library, San Marino, CA.

[6] "Provisional Outline," n.d. Huntington Library, San Marino, CA.

[7] Letter to Diane Cleaver, 25 April 1972. Huntington Library, San Marino, CA.

[8] Letter to Larry Ashmead, 4 July 1973. Huntington Library, San Marino, CA.

[9] Griffin and Wingrove, 162; citing *BYS,* 317.

[10] A fuller discussion of *This World* was published in the *Science Fiction Research Association Newsletter,* 96 (November 1981), 6-9.

XIV
Selectively Annotated Primary Bibliography

I. NOVELS AND POETRY

An Age. London: Faber, 1967. (Republished as *Cryptozoic!*. New York: Doubleday, 1967.) The experiences of Edward Bush, a 21st-century, mind-traveling artist, whose pursuit of Professor Silverstone leads to a startling theory of time and history.

Barefoot in the Head: A European Fantasia. London: Faber, 1969; New York: Doubleday, 1970. Aldiss' experiment in Joycean prose. Colin Charteris travels through a Europe suffering hallucinations and distorted perceptions resulting from the Acid War.

Bow Down to Nul. New York: Ace, 1960. (Retitled *The Interpreter.* London: Digit, 1961. See also "X for Exploitation.") Gary Towler leads a group of patriots in their attempts to rid the Earth of the alien Nuls.

The Brightfount Diaries. London: Faber, 1955. Aldiss' first novel, a non-SF portrayal of life in a bookseller's shop.

Brothers of the Head. London: Pierrot, 1977; New York: Two Continents, 1978. A psychological study of the lives and deaths of rock musicians Barry and Tom Howe, Siamese twins struggling for dominance between themselves and with a somnolent third head growing from Barry's shoulder.

Cryptozoic!. See *An Age.*

The Dark Light Years. London: Faber, 1964; New York: Signet, 1964. Human space-explorers capture aliens whose technology, psychology, and philosophy highlight failings in human society.

Earthworks: A Science Fiction Novel. London: Faber, 1965; New York: Doubleday, 1966. Knowle Noland struggles for meaning in a disintegrating society on an overpopulated Earth whose only hope lies (perhaps) in nuclear war.

The Eighty-Minute Hour: A Space Opera. London: Cape, 1974; New York: Doubleday, 1974. Aldiss' wildly inventive homage to space opera, incorporating a post-war Earth, extraordinary scientific possibilities, and bizarre characters, topped with verbal play and operatic songs.

Enemies of the System: A Tale of Homo Uniformis. London: Cape, 1978; New York: Harper, 1978. Six members of the elite, celebrating the millionth anniversary of Biocom (biological communism), are stranded in the wilds of Lysenka II, where they and their socio-political theories are tested.

Equator. See *Vanguard from Alpha.*

Farewell to a Child. Berkhamsted, Hertfordshire: Priapus Press, 1982. (Poetry).

Frankenstein Unbound. London: Cape, 1973; New York: Random House, 1973. Joseph Bodenland time-slips from the year 2020 to 1816 and meets Mary Shelley, Victor Frankenstein, *and* Frankenstein's monster. An indictment of the twentieth-century myth of technological progress.

Greybeard. London: Faber, 1964; New York: Harcourt, 1964. Algy Timberlake embarks on an odyssey through an England without children, where the youngest humans are in their fifties and sixties. Through flashbacks, Aldiss reveals the nature of the Accident that sterilized most of humanity.

The Hand-Reared Boy. London: Weidenfeld & Nicolson, 1970. The first of Aldiss' best-selling Horatio Stubbs novels details the emerging sexual awareness of young Stubbs.

Helliconia Spring. London: Cape, 1982; New York: Atheneum, 1982. Volume one of Aldiss' monumental study of change and adaptation on a planet whose Great Year of 2592 Earth years creates extraordinary climatic cycles. In *Spring,* civilization begins to restructure itself after a centuries-long winter.

Helliconia Summer. London: Cape, 1983; New York: Atheneum, 1983. Volume two of the Helliconia series. King JandolAnganol fights for stability within personal, social, political, and religious turmoil, complicated by the increasingly unbearable heat of Helliconian summer.

Helliconia Winter. London: Cape, 1985; New York: Atheneum, 1985. In the concluding volume, Luterin Shokerandit and his world face the return of Helliconian winter and the disintegration of their society and culture.

Hothouse: A Science Fiction Novel. London: Faber, 1962 (Reprinted as *The Long Afternoon of Earth.* New York: Signet, 1962). The exploits of Gren and his fellow humans on a dying Earth where vegetable-forms have supplanted mammalian as dominant species.

An Island Called Moreau. See *Moreau's Other Island.*

The Interpreter. See *Bow Down to Nul.*

Life in the West. London: Weidenfeld & Nicolson, 1980. Non-SF novel dealing with the personal and public problems faced by Thomas Squire. The portrayal of the state of Western civilization in the late seventies is an effective prelude to Helliconia.

The Long Afternoon of Earth. See *Hothouse.*

The Malacia Tapestry. London: Cape, 1976; New York: Harper & Row, 1977. The adventures of Perian de Chirolo in pseudo-Renaissance Malacia, a city-state protected from change by the Original Curse.

The Male Response: A Timely Original Story. New York: Galaxy, 1961; London: Dennis Dobson, 1963. Non-SF. Soames Noyes travels to Africa to install a computer. Once there, he finds more outlets for his energies and interests than mere technology.

Moreau's Other Island. London: Cape, 1980 (Retitled *An Island Called Moreau.* New York: Simon & Schuster, 1981). Following the sabotage of his space capsule, Calvert Roberts lands on an island inhabited by strange half-human, half-beast natives under the control of Mortimer Dart, a thalilomide baby who supplements his deformed limbs with robotic prostheses.

Non-Stop. London: Faber, 1958 (Retitled *Starship.* New York: Criterion, 1959). Roy Complain searches the passageways of his spaceship-world to discover who he is, what his world is like, and where it is bound. Aldiss' first published SF novel.

Pile: Petals From St Klaed's Computer. New York: Holt, Rinehart and Winston, 1979. Illus. Mike Wilks. Poetry. Beautifully illustrated volume. Aldiss' poem details the adventures of Lord Scart, who brings change to the computer-regulated city of Pile.

The Primal Urge. New York: Ballantine, 1961; London: Sphere, 1967 (See also "Minor Operation"). A marginally SF novel detailing James Solent's responses as part of a society under the influence of ERs (Emotional Registers), implants in the forehead which "pink" when the wearer is sexually aroused.

Report on Probability A. London: Faber, 1968; Garden City, NY: Doubleday, 1969. Aldiss' "anti-novel," a stylistic experiment concentrating on G, S, and C as they watch Mr. and Mrs. Mary's house, unaware that they are in turn the subject of level after level of unseen observers. An exploration of objectivity and perspective.

A Rude Awakening. London: Weidenfeld & Nicolson, 1978; New York: Random House, 1979. Non-SF. The third Stubbs novel, a semi-autobiographical account of Stubbs' experiences with love and war in Sumatra in 1946.

A Soldier Erect: Being the Further Adventures of the Hand-Reared Boy. London: Weidenfeld & Nicolson, 1971; New York: Coward McCann, 1971. The second Stubbs novel, in which Stubbs, now in the army and stationed in India, continues his sexual adventures.

Starship. See *Non-Stop.*

Vanguard From Alpha. London: Digit, 1958 (Reprinted as *Equator* with "Segregation." New York: Ace, 1959). Humans versus alien invaders in a SF adventure.

II. COLLECTIONS OF ALDISS' SHORT FICTION

The Airs of Earth: Science Fiction Stories. London: Faber, 1963.

Best of Aldiss. In *Bestseller,* 3, no. 9 (1983). Ed. Deborah Musselwhite. A magazine devoted to Aldiss' short fiction; the first time the series has included a science-fiction writer.

Best Science-Fiction Stories of Brian W. Aldiss. London: Faber, 1965 (Retitled *Who Can Replace a Man? The Best Science-Fiction Stories of Brian W. Aldiss.* New York: Harcourt Brace, 1966).

Best Science-Fiction Stories of Brian W. Aldiss (rev. ed.). London: Faber, 1971.

The Book of Brian Aldiss. New York: DAW, 1972 (Retitled *The Comic Inferno.* London: Sidgwick & Jackson, 1973).

A Brian Aldiss Omnibus. London: Sidgwick & Jackson, 1969.

Brian Aldiss Omnibus (2). London: Sidgwick & Jackson, 1971.

The Canopy of Time. London: Faber, 1959.

Foreign Bodies. Singapore: Chopmen, 1981.

Galaxies Like Grains of Sand. New York: Signet, 1960 (based on *The Canopy of Time*).

Intangibles, Inc., and Other Stories: Five Novellas. London: Faber, 1969.

Last Orders and Other Stories. London: Cape, 1977.

The Moment of Eclipse. London: Faber, 1970; New York: Doubleday, 1972.

Neanderthal Planet. New York: Avon, 1970.

New Arrivals, Old Encounters. London: Cape, 1979; New York: Harper & Row, 1979.

No Time Like Tomorrow. New York: Signet, 1959 (adapted from *Space, Time and Nathaniel*).

The Saliva Tree, and Other Strange Growths. London: Faber, 1966.

Seasons in Flight. London: Cape, 1984.

Space, Time and Nathaniel (Presciences). London: Faber: 1957. Aldiss' first collection.

Starswarm. New York: Signet, 1964 (adapted from *The Airs of Earth*).

Who Can Replace a Man? The Best Science-Fiction Stories of Brian W. Aldiss. New York: Harcourt, 1966. Reprint of *Best Science-Fiction Stories of Brian W. Aldiss.*

III. EDITED ANTHOLOGIES

Best Fantasy Stories. London: Faber, 1962.

Evil Earths. London: Weidenfeld & Nicolson, 1975. Third in Space Opera series.

Galactic Empires, I. London: Weidenfeld & Nicolson, 1976; New York: St. Martin's, 1977. Fourth in the Space Opera series.

Galactic Empires, II. London: Weidenfeld & Nicolson, 1976; New York; St. Martin's, 1977.

Introducing SF: A Science Fiction Anthology. London: Faber, 1964.

More Penguin Science Fiction: An Anthology. Harmondsworth: Penguin, 1963.

Penguin Science Fiction: An Anthology. Harmondsworth: Penguin, 1961.

The Penguin Science Fiction Omnibus: An Anthology. Harmondsworth: Penguin: 1973.

Perilous Planets. London: Weidenfeld & Nicolson, 1978: New York: Avon, 1978.

Space Odysseys: A New Look at Yesterday's Futures. London: Orbit, 1974; New York: Doubleday, 1976. Second in Space Opera series.

Space Opera: An Anthology of Way-Back-When Futures. London: Orbit, 1974; New York: Doubleday, 1975.

Yet More Penguin Science Fiction. Harmondsworth: Penguin, 1964.

WITH HARRY HARRISON

All About Venus: A Revelation of the Planet Venus in Fact and Fiction. New York: Dell, 1968. (Abridged reprint of *Farewell, Fantastic Venus.*)

The Astounding-Analog Reader. Vol. I. New York: Doubleday, 1972. (Abridged and retitled *The Astounding-Analog Reader, Book 1.* London: Sphere, 1973.)

The Astounding-Analog Reader, Vol. II. New York: Doubleday, 1973. (Abridged and retitled *The Astounding-Analog Reader, Book 2.* London: Sphere, 1973.)

Best SF: 1967. New York: Berkley, 1968. (Retitled *The Year's Best Science Fiction, No. 1*).

Best SF: 1968. New York: Putnams, 1969.

Best SF: 1969. New York: Putnams, 1970.

Best SF: 1970. New York: Putnams, 1971.

Best SF: 1971. New York: Putnams, 1972.

Best SF: 1972. New York: Putnams, 1973.

Best SF: 1973. New York: Putnams, 1974.

Best SF: 1974. Indianapolis: Bobbs-Merrill, 1975.

Best SF: 1975. Indianapolis: Bobbs-Merrill, 1976.

Decade the 1940s. London: Macmillan, 1975; New York: St. Martin's, 1978.

Decade the 1950s. London: Macmillan, 1976; New York: St. Martin's, 1978.

Decade the 1960s. London: Macmillan, 1977.

Farewell, Fantastic Venus: A History of the Planet Venus in Fact and Fiction. London: Macdonald, 1968. See *All About Venus.*

Nebula Award Stories Two. New York: Doubleday, 1967; London: Gollancz, 1967.

The Year's Best Science Fiction, No. 1. London: Sphere, 1968. See *Best SF: 1967.*

The Year's Best Science Fiction, No. 2. London: Sphere, 1969. See *Best SF: 1968.*

The Year's Best Science Fiction, No. 3. London: Sphere, 1970. See *Best SF: 1969.*

The Year's Best Science Fiction, No. 4. London: Sphere: 1971. See *Best SF: 1970.*

The Year's Best Science Fiction, No. 5. London: Sphere, 1972. See *Best SF: 1971.*

The Year's Best Science Fiction, No. 6. London: Sphere, 1973.

IV. SHORT FICTION

"An Age." *New Worlds SF,* October 1967, pp. 5-14; November 1967, pp. 8-29; December 1967, pp. 43-58.

"Ahead." See "The Failed Men."

"Aimez-vous Holman Hunt." See "The Aperture Moment."

"All The World's Tears." *Nebula,* May 1957, pp. 24-35.

"All Those Enduring Old Charms." See "The Eternal Theme of Exile."

"Always Somebody There." In *Tomorrow: New Worlds of Science Fiction.* Ed. Roger Elwood. New York: Evans, 1976.

"Amen and Out." *New Worlds SF,* August 1966, pp. 5-24.

"An Appearance of Life." See "Appearance of Life."

"And the Stagnation of the Heart." *New Worlds SF,* December 1968, pp. 4-9.

"Another Little Boy." *New Worlds SF,* September 1966, pp. 103-116.

"The Aperture Moment." In *Epoch.* Ed. Roger Elwood and Robert Silverberg. New York: Berkley, 1975, pp. 437-462. Includes: "Waiting for the Universe to Begin," "But Without Orifices," "Aimez-vous Holman Hunt."

"Appearance of Life." In *Andromeda 1.* Ed. Peter Weston. London: Futura, 1976, pp. 9-24; as "An Appearance of Life," in *Best of Aldiss.* Ed. Deborah Musselwhite. *Bestsellers,* 3, no. 9 (1983), 10-15. The Aldiss issue represents the first time *Bestsellers* has honored a science-fiction writer.

"Are You an Android?" *Science Fantasy,* April 1959, pp. 105-109.

"The Arm." *Nebula,* January 1959, pp. 21-29.

"As For Our Fatal Continuity." In *New Worlds Quarterly, 3.* Ed. Michael Moorcock. London: Sphere, 1972; New York: Berkley, 1972, pp. 39-43.

"Auto-Ancestral Fracture." *New Worlds SF,* December 1967, pp. 19-30. Incorporated into *Barefoot in the Head.*

"Backwater." *Ambit 69,* London, 1967.

"Basis for Negotiation." *New Worlds SF,* January 1962, pp. 50-90.

"Blighted Profile." *Science Fantasy,* June 1958, pp. 93-102.

"The Blue Background." *Isaac Asimov's Science Fiction Magazine* (1983); In *Best of Aldiss.* Ed. Deborah Musselwhite. *Bestsellers,* 3, no. 9 (1983), pp. 40-44.

"The Bomb-Proof Bomb." *Oxford Times,* 10 April 1959.

"The Bones of Bertram Russell." In *New Writings in Science Fiction 28.* Ed. Kenneth Bulmer. London: Sidgwick & Jackson, 1976, pp. 69-78.

"A Book in Time." *The Bookseller,* 13 February 1954.

"Breathing Space." *Science Fantasy,* February 1955, pp. 116-128.

"Burning Question." *Fantasy and Science Fiction,* October 1966, pp. 101–110.

"But Who Can Replace a Man?" *Infinity Science Fiction,* June 1958, pp. 58–67.

"But Without Orifices." See "The Aperture Moment."

"Cardiac Arrest." *Fantastic.* December 1970, pp. 60–79, 140. Novelette.

"Carefully Observed Women." See "Three Coins in an Enigmatic Fountain."

"The Carp That Once." *Science Fantasy,* April 1958, pp. 107–111.

"Carrion Country." *New Worlds SF,* November 1958, pp. 45–68.

"Castle Scene With Penitents." In *Orbit 12.* Ed. Damon Knight. New York: Putnams, 1973, 113–131. Incorporated into *The Malacia Tapestry.*

"The Circulation of the Blood." *Impulse,* March 1966, pp. 4–35. Novelette.

"Comic Inferno." *Galaxy,* February 1963, pp. 92–129. Novella.

"Confluence." *Punch,* 30 August 1967, pp. 297–299.

"Consolations of Age." In *Best of Aldiss.* Ed. Deborah Musselwhite. *Bestsellers,* 3, no. 9 (1983), 55–56.

"Conversation Piece." *New Worlds SF,* February 1962, pp. 56–65.

"Conviction." *New Worlds SF,* September 1956, pp. 45–57.

"Counter-feat." *New Worlds SF,* February 1964, pp. 49–56.

"Creatures of Apogee." In *New Writings in SF, 31.* Ed. Kenneth Bulmer. London: Sidgwick & Jackson, 1977.

"Criminal Record." *Science Fantasy,* July 1954, pp. 54–62.

"The Cultural Side-Effect." See "Diagrams for Three Enigmatic Stories."

"The Daffodil Returns the Smile." See "Three Enigmas IV."

"Danger: Religion." See "Matrix."

"The Dark Light-Years." *Worlds of Tomorrow,* April 1964, pp. 7–104. Short novel.

"The Dark Night of the Soul." In *The Ides of Tomorrow.* Ed. Terry Carr. Boston: Little Brown, 1976, pp. 34–47.

"The Day of the Doomed King." *Science Fantasy,* November 1965, pp. 5–19.

"The Day We Embarked for Cythera." In *New Worlds Quarterly, 1.* Ed. Michael Moorcock. London: Sphere, 1971; New York: Berkley, 1971.

"The Dead Immortal." *Titbits,* 20 May 1967.

"Diagram for Three Enigmatic Stories." In *Final Stages.* Ed. Edward Ferrman and Barry Malzberg. New York: Charterhouse, 1974, pp. 62–88. Includes "The Girl in the Tau-dream," "The Immobility Crew," "The Cultural Side-Effect."

"A Difficult Age." *Nova,* Christmas Issue (November 1967), pp. 114–115.

"Down the Up Escalation." *London Magazine,* February 1967, pp. 58–65.

"The Drake-Man Route." *New Worlds SF,* July 1968, pp. 12–19. Incorporated into *Barefoot in the Head.*

"Dreamer, Schemer." *Galaxy,* July 1968, pp. 125–135.

"Dumb Show." *Nebula*, December 1956, pp. 22–28.
"The Enigma of Her Voyage." See "Three Enigmas."
"Equator I." *New Worlds SF*, September 1958, pp. 4–41; October 1958, pp. 80–121.
"The Ergot Show." In *Nova 2*. Ed. Harry Harrison. New York: Walker, 1972, pp. 193–209.
"The Eternal Theme of Exile." In *New Writings in Science Fiction*, 23. Ed. Kenneth Bulmer. London: Sidgwick & Jackson, 1974, pp. 81–90. Includes "The Eternal Theme of Exile," "All Those Enduring Old Charms," "Nobody Spoke or Waved Goodbye."
"Evergreen." *Fantasy and Science Fiction*, December 1961, pp. 82–130. Incorporated into *Hothouse*.
"The Eyes of the Blind King." *Impulse*, November 1960, pp. 98–118.
"The Expensive Delicate Ship." In *Nova 3*. Ed. Harry Harrison. New York: Walker, 1973, pp. 23–29.
"Faceless Card." *Science Fantasy*, April 1960, pp. 52–69.
"The Failed Men." *Science Fantasy*, May 1956, pp. 83–109. Retitled "Ahead."
"The Firmament Theorem." *New Worlds SF*, June 1969, pp. 49–57.
"Flowers of the Forest." *Science Fantasy*, August 1957, pp. 34–44.
"Fortune's Fool." *Science Fantasy*, June 1959, pp. 80–88.
"Four Stories." In *Orbit 12*. See "Serpent Burning on an Altar," "Woman in Sunlight with Mandolin," "The Young Soldier's Horoscope," "Castle Scene with Penitents."
"Fourth Factor." *Nebula*, September 1958, pp. 3–26; *Original Science Fiction Stories*, September 1958, pp. 48–74. Novelette.
"Full Sun." In *Orbit 2*. Ed. Damon Knight. New York: Putnams, 1967, pp. 241–255.
"The Game of God." See "Segregation."
"The Game With the Big Heavy Ball." In *New Writings in SF*, 30. Ed. Kenneth Bulmer. London: Sidgwick & Jackson, 1978; *Best of Aldiss*. Ed. Deborah Musselwhite, *Bestsellers*, 9, no. 3 (1983), pp. 20–23.
"The Gene-Hive." See "Journey to the Interior."
"Gesture of Farewell." *New Worlds SF*, July 1957, pp. 70–93.
"Girl and Robot with Flowers." *New Worlds SF*, September 1965, pp. 5–11.
"The Girl in the Tau-dream." See "Diagram for Three Enigmatic Stories."
"The Girl Who Sang." In *Best of Aldiss*. Ed. Deborah Musselwhite, *Bestsellers*, 3, no. 9 (1983), pp. 57–64.
"The Great Chain of Being What?" See "Three Enigmas."
"The Great Time Hiccup." *Nebula*, April 1965, pp. 66–74.
"Greeks Bringing Knee-High Gifts." *Galaxy*, March 1969, pp. 147–152.
"The Green Leaves of Space." *Daily Express Science Annual*, 1 (1962), pp. 66–77.
"Have Your Hatreds Ready." *Fantasy and Science Fiction*, May 1958, pp. 90–104. Retitled "Secret of a Mighty City."

"Hearts and Engines." See "Soldiers Running."

"Hen's Eyes." *Amazing,* September 1961, pp. 34–52. Novelette.

"Heresies of the Huge God." *Galaxy,* August 1966, pp. 34–43.

"Horseman." *Cosmos,* September 1977, pp. 48–50. Retitled "New Arrivals, Old Encounters."

"Hothouse." *Fantasy and Science Fiction,* February 1961, pp. 5–35. Incorporated into *Hothouse.*

"How to Be a Soldier." See "Soldiers Running."

"The Humming Heads." *Solstice,* June 1969, pp. 31–35.

"The Hunter at His Ease." In *Science Against Man.* Ed. Anthony Cheetham. New York: Avon, 1970, pp. 77–96.

"The Ice Mass Cometh." *Oxford Mail,* 1 December 1957; *New Worlds SF,* December 1967, pp. 93–95.

"I Ching, Who You?" See "Three Enigmas."

"I Dreamed I Was Jung Last Night." See "When I Was Very Jung."

"The Immobility Crew." See "Diagram for Three Enigmatic Stories."

"The Impossible Star." *Worlds of Tomorrow,* August 1963, pp. 143–162.

"Incentive." *New Worlds SF,* December 1958, pp. 83–97.

"Index to Life." *The Bookseller* (1954).

"Indifference." In *Rooms of Parades.* Ed. Lee Harding. Melbourne: Quartet Books, 1978, pp. 1–24.

"In the Arena." *If, Worlds of Science Fiction,* July 1963, pp. 80–88.

"In the Mist of Life." In *Winter's Tales,* 23. Ed. Peter Collenette. London: Macmillan, 1977, pp. 9–17.

"Intangibles, Inc." *Science Fantasy,* February 1959, pp. 110–128.

"The International Smile." In *Airs of Earth.*

"The Interpreter." In *A Brian Aldiss Omnibus.* See "X for Exploitation."

"Journey to Heartland." In *Universe 6.* Ed. Terry Carr. New York: Doubleday, 1976.

"Journey to the Interior." *Nebula,* May 1958, pp. 3–20. Retitled "The Gene-Hive."

"Judas Dancing." *Star Science Fiction,* January 1958, pp. 78–92; as "Judas Danced." *Science Fantasy,* February 1958, pp. 44–57.

"Jungle Substitute." *Galaxy,* August 1964, pp. 92–117.

"Just Passing Through." *Impulse,* February 1967, pp. 17–29. Incorporated into *Barefoot in the Head.*

"Killing Off the Big Animals." See "Year By Year the Evil Gains."

"A Kind of Artistry." *Fantasy and Science Fiction,* October 1962, pp. 6–27, 150.

"Lambeth Blossoms." *Knight,* September 1966, pp. 10–13, etc.

"Last Orders." *SF Digest,* 1 (1976), 31–35.

"Legends of Smith's Burst." *Nebula,* June 1959, pp. 66–105.

"Let's Be Frank." *Science Fantasy,* June 1957, pp. 84–92.

"The Lieutenant." *Nebula,* February 1959, pp. 62–73.

"Listen With Big Brother." *Punch,* 2–8. January 1974, pp. 14–16. Retitled "Wired for Sound."

"Live? Our Computers Will Do That For Us." In *Orbit 15*. Ed. Damon Knight. New York: Harper & Row, 1974, pp. 130-148.

"The Lonely Habit." *Ellery Queen*, June 1966, pp. 121-127.

"Looking on the Sunny Side of an Eclipse." See "Three Enigmas III."

"Man in His Time." *Science Fantasy*, April 1965, pp. 5-32.

"Man on Bridge." In *New Writings in Science Fiction*, 1. Ed. John Carnell. London: Dobson, 1964.

"Manuscript Found in a Police State." In *Winter's Tale*, 18. Ed. A. D. Maclean. New York: Macmillan, 1972, pp. 9-40.

"Matrix." *Science Fantasy*, October 1962, pp. 2-39.

"Melancholia Has a Plastic Core." *Sf Monthly*, 1 (1974).

"Minor Operation." *New Worlds SF*, June 1962, pp. 4-54; July 1962, pp. 57-124; August 1962, pp. 73-128. See *The Primal Urge*.

"Modernisation." In *Winter's Tales*, 26. Ed. A. D. Maclean. London: Macmillan, 1980.

"The Moment of Eclipse." *New Worlds SF*, May 1969, pp. 4-12.

"The Monster of Ingratitude IV." In *Nova 4*. Ed. Harry Harrison. New York: Walker, 1974, pp. 1-9.

"Moon of Delight." *New Worlds SF*, March 1961, pp. 4-32. Retitled "O Moon of My Delight."

"Multi-Value Motorway." *New Worlds SF*, August 1967, pp. 46-53. Incorporated into *Barefoot in the Head*.

"My Lady of the Psychiatric Sorrows." In *Universe 7*. Ed. Terry Carr. New York: Doubleday, 1977.

"Neanderthal Planet." See "A Touch of Neanderthal."

"Never Let Go of My Hand." *New Worlds SF*, May/June 1964, pp. 48-66.

"New Arrivals, Old Encounters." See "Horsemen."

"The New Father Christmas." *Fantasy and Science Fiction*, January 1958, pp. 69-74.

"The Night That All Time Broke Out." In *Dangerous Visions*. Ed. Harlan Ellison. New York: Doubleday, 1967, pp. 157-168.

"Ninian's Experiences." *Nebula*, June 1958, pp. 16-26.

"Nipples as an Index of Character." *Commentary* (Singapore), 1976.

"Nobody Spoke or Waved Goodbye." See "The Eternal Theme of Exile."

"No Gimmick." *Science Fantasy*, February 1957, pp. 73-85.

"Nomansland." *Fantasy and Science Fiction*, April 1961, pp. 99-130. Incorporated into *Hothouse*.

"Non-Isotropic." *Galileo*, March 1978, pp. 41-43.

"Non-Stop." *Science Fantasy*, February 1956, pp. 2-38. Novelette.

"Not for an Age." *The London Observer*, 9 January 1955.

"O Moon of My Delight." See "Moon of Delight."

"Oh For a Closer Brush With God." *20 Houses of the Zodiac*, 1978; In *Best of Aldiss*. Ed. Deborah Musselwhite, *Bestsellers*, 9, no. 3 (1983), 3-9.

"The Oh In Jose." *Cad*, March 1966, pp. 50-55; *Impulse*, July 1966, pp.

69-79.

"Oh Ishrael." *New Worlds SF,* April 1957, pp. 61-73.

"The Old and Fleeting Images." See "Three Enigmas III."

"Old Hundredth." *New Worlds SF,* November 1960, pp. 62-80.

"Old Time's Sake." *New Worlds SF,* September 1965, pp. 12-25.

"One Blink of the Moon." In *New Arrivals, Old Encounters.*

"One Role With Relish." In *The Saliva Tree and Other Strange Growths.*

"One-Way Strait." *New Worlds SF,* February 1964, pp. 57-64.

"Orgy of the Living and the Dying." In *The Year 2000.* Ed. Harry Harrison. New York: Doubleday, 1970; New York: Berkley, 1970, pp. 101-132.

"Original Sinner." *Science Fiction Adventures,* July 1960, pp. 85-130.

"The Other One." *New Worlds SF,* April 1959, pp. 44-68.

"Our Kind of Knowledge." *New Worlds SF,* June 1955, pp. 73-85.

"Ouspenski's Astrabahn." *New Worlds SF,* January 1969, pp. 36-53. Novella. Incorporated into *Barefoot in the Head.*

"Out of Reach." *Authentic Science Fiction,* August 1957, pp. 78-90.

"Outside." *New Worlds SF,* January 1955, pp. 29-37.

"Panel Game." *New Worlds SF,* December 1955, pp. 63-72.

"Patagonia's Delicious Filling Station." In *New Worlds Nine* [Quarterly]. Ed. Hilary Bailey. London: Corgi, 1975.

"Paternal Care." In *The Saliva Tree and Other Strange Growths.*

"Pink Plastic Gods." *Science Fantasy,* June/July 1964, pp. 5-21.

"The Pit My Parish." *New Worlds SF,* January 1958, pp. 43-62.

"Planet of Death." *New Worlds SF* [American reprint], July 1960, pp. 32-75. See "Segregation."

"A Pleasure Shared." *Rogue,* December 1962, pp. 24-25.

"Pogsmith." *Authentic Science Fiction,* May 1955, pp. 57-69.

"Poor Little Warrior!" *Fantasy and Science Fiction,* April 1958, pp. 125-130.

"The Primal Urge." In *A Brian Aldiss Omnibus.* See "Minor Operation."

"A Private Whale." In *Perpetual Light.* Ed. Alan Ryan. New York: Warner, 1983, pp. 407-435.

"Psyclops." *New Worlds SF,* July 1956, pp. 30-39.

"Randy's Syndrome." *Fantasy and Science Fiction,* April 1967, pp. 111-130.

"Report on Probability A." *New Worlds SF,* February 1967, pp. 4-113.

"Safety Valve." *Future Science Fiction,* August 1959, pp. 6-27.

"The Saliva Tree." *Fantasy and Science Fiction,* September 1965, pp. 4-54.

"Scarfe's World." *Worlds of Tomorrow,* March 1965, pp. 104-117.

"Secret of a Mighty City." See "Have Your Hatreds Ready."

"Segregation." *New Worlds SF,* July 1958, pp. 4-47. Retitled "The Game of God," "Planet of Death."

"Send Her Victorious." *Amazing,* April 1968, pp. 4-36.

"Serpent Burning on an Altar." In *Orbit 12.* Ed. Damon Knight. New

York: Putnams, 1973, pp. 60-76. Incorporated into *The Malacia Tapestry.*

"Serpent of the Kundalini." *New Worlds SF,* February 1968, pp. 26-32. Incorporated into *Barefoot in the Head.*

"Shards." *Fantasy and Science Fiction,* April 1962, pp. 49-56.

"The Shubshub Race." In *Space, Time, and Nathaniel.*

"Sight of a Silhouette." *Nebula,* November 1958, pp. 40-50.

"Since the Assassination." In *Intangibles, Inc., and Other Stories.*

"Skeleton Crew." *Science Fantasy,* December 1963, pp. 2-95. See *Earthworks.*

"The Small Betraying Detail." *New Worlds SF,* May 1965, pp. 39-48.

"The Small Stones of Tu Fu." *Isaac Asimov's Science Fiction Magazine,* March/April 1978, pp. 43-51.

"So Far From Prague." In *The New S. F.* Ed. Langdon Jones. London: Hutchinson, 1969, pp. 55-70.

"Sober Noises of Morning in a Marginal Land." In *Best Science Fiction Stories of Brian W. Aldiss.*

"The Soft Predicament." *Fantasy and Science Fiction,* October 1969, pp. 62-86.

"Soldiers Running." *New Worlds SF,* June 1960, pp. 94-104. Retitled "Hearts and Engines," "How to Be a Soldier."

"The Song of the Silencer." In *New Arrivals, Old Encounters.*

"The Source." *New Worlds SF,* August 1965, pp. 61-74.

"A Space for Reflection." In *New Writings in Science Fiction, 29.* Ed. Kenneth Bulmer. London: Sidgwick & Jackson, 1976, pp. 73-92.

"A Spot of Konfrontation." *Penthouse,* April 1973, pp. 55-58.

"Stage-Struck." *Science Fantasy,* June 1960, pp. 84-128.

"Still Trajectories." *New Worlds SF,* September 1967, pp. 22-29. Incorporated into *Barefoot in the Head.*

"Strange in a Familiar Way." In *Beyond This Horizon.* Ed. Christopher Carnell. Sunderland: Ceolfrith, 1973, pp. 29-33.

"Supercity." In *Space, Time, and Nathaniel.*

"Super-Toys Last All Summer Long." *Harper's Bazaar,* December 1969, pp. 70-72.

"Swastika!" In *Nova One.* Ed. Harry Harrison. New York: Dell, 1970, pp. 73-81.

"T." *Nebula,* November 1956, pp. 20-25.

"A Taste for Dostoyevsky." In *New Writings in Science Fiction, 10.* Ed. John Carnell. London: Dobson, 1967, pp. 121-140.

"The Tell-Tale Heart-Machine." *Galaxy,* November 1968, pp. 153-158.

"Ten Storey Jigsaw." *Nebula,* January 1958, pp. 54-61.

"That Uncomfortable Pause Between Life and Art." *Queen,* July 1969, pp. 50-51.

"There is a Tide." *New Worlds SF,* February 1956, pp. 80-93.

"They Shall Inherit." *Nebula,* July 1958, pp. 48-56.

"The Thing Under the Glacier." In *Daily Express Science Annual 2,*

September 1963, pp. 69-80.

"Three Coins in Enigmatic Fountains." See "Three Enigmas IV."

"Three Deadly Enigmas: Year by Year the Evil Gains." In *New Writings in Science Fiction.* Ed. Kenneth Bulmer. London: Sidgwick & Jackson, 1975, pp. 71-92. Includes "XIII. Within the Black Circle," "XIV. Killing Off the Big Animals," "XV. What Are You Doing, Why Are You Doing It?"

"Three Enigmas, I." In *New Writings in Science Fiction,* 22. Ed. Kenneth Bulmer. London: Sidgwick & Jackson, 1973, pp. 67-72. Includes "I. The Enigma of Her Voyage," "II. I Ching, Who You?," "III. The Great Chain of Being What?"

"Three Enigmas, II: The Eternal Theme of Exile." In *New Writings in Science Fiction,* 23. Ed. Kenneth Bulmer. London: Sidgwick & Jackson, 1974, pp. 81-90. Includes "The Eternal Theme of Exile," "All Those Enduring Old Charms," "Nobody Spoke or Waved Goodbye."

"Three Enigmas, III: All In God's Mind." In *New Writings in Science Fiction,* 24. Ed. Kenneth Bulmer. London: Sidgwick & Jackson, 1974. Includes "VII. The Unbearableness of Other Lives," "VIII. The Old and Fleeting Images," "IX. Looking on the Sunny Side of an Eclipse."

"Three Enigmas, IV: Three Coins in Enigmatic Fountains." In *New Writings in Science Fiction,* 26. Ed. Kenneth Bulmer. London: Sidgwick & Jackson, 1976, pp. 51-66. Includes "X. Carefully Observed Women," "XI. The Daffodil Returns the Smile," "XII. The Year of the Quiet Computer."

"Three Revolutionary Enigmas." In *Something Else,* 1, 1980: *Best of Aldiss.* Ed. Deborah Musselwhite, *Bestsellers,* 9, no. 3 (1983), pp. 29-39. Includes "The Fall of Species B," "In the Halls of the Hereafter," "The Ancestral Home of Thought." Also "Three Evolutionary Enigmas."

"Three's a Cloud." See "The Unbeaten Track."

"Three Songs for Enigmatic Lovers." In *The Shape of Sex to Come,* 1974.

"Three Ways." *Fantasy and Science Fiction.* In *New Arrivals, Old Encounters.*

"Timberline." *Fantasy and Science Fiction,* September 1961, pp. 99-129. Incorporated into *Hothouse.*

"Total Environment." *Galaxy,* February 1968, pp. 113-156.

"A Touch of Neanderthal." *Science Fiction Adventures,* September 1960, pp. 2-27. See "Neanderthal Planet."

"The Towers of San Ampa." *New Worlds SF,* February 1959, pp. 24-38.

"Tradesman's Exit." *The Bookseller,* 14 January 1956.

"Tyrant's Territory." *Amazing,* March 1962, pp. 106-128.

"The Unbearableness of Other Lives." See "Three Enigmas III: All in God's Mind."

"The Unbeaten Track." *New Worlds SF,* January 1959, pp. 24-30. Re-

titled "Three's a Cloud."
"Under an English Heaven." *New Worlds SF,* January 1960, pp. 39-52.
"Undergrowth." *Fantasy and Science Fiction,* July 1961, pp. 84-129.
Incorporated into *Hothouse.*
"The Under-Privileged." *New Worlds SF,* May 1963, pp. 26-41.
"The Village Swindler." *International,* October 1968, 20-25.
"Visiting Amoeba." See "What Triumphs."
"Waiting for the Universe to Begin." See "The Aperture Moment."
"The Weather on Demansky Island." *Quicksilver,* December 1970.
"What Triumphs?" *Authentic Science Fiction,* July 1957, pp. 4-34. Retitled "Visiting Amoeba."
"What Are You Doing, Why Are You Doing It?" See "Three Deadly Enigmas V: Year By Year the Evil Gains."
"What You Get For Your Dollar." In *The New Improved Sun.* Ed. Thomas Disch. New York: Harper, 1976, pp. 37-48.
"When I Was Very Jung." *Galaxy,* September 1968, pp. 56-60.
"Where the Lines Converge." *Galileo,* April 1967; In *Strangeness.* Ed. Thomas Disch and C. Naylor. New York: Scribners, 1977. Published with *Brothers of the Head.*
"Who Can Replace a Man?" See "But Who Can Replace a Man?"
"Wired for Sound." See "Listen With Big Brother."
"With Esmond in Mind." *Science Fantasy,* December 1956, pp. 83-95.
"Within the Black Circle." See "Three Deadly Enigmas: V: Year By Year the Evil Gains."
"Woman in Sunlight With Mandolin." In *Orbit 12.* Ed. Damon Knight. New York: Putnams, 1973, pp. 77-88. Incorporated into *The Malacia Tapestry.*
"Wonder Weapons." *Nova,* Christmas Issue (November 1967), pp. 119-123.
"Working in the Spaceship Yards." *Punch,* April 1969, 519-521.
"The Worm That Flies." In *The Farthest Reaches.* Ed. Joseph Elder. New York: Trident, 1968, pp. 15-38.
"X For Exploitation." *New Worlds SF,* March 1960, pp. 4-42; April 1960, pp. 78-123; May 1960, pp. 78-123. Retitled *Bow Down to Nul,* and *The Interpreter.*
"Year By Year the Evil Gains." See "Three Deadly Enigmas V: Year By Year the Evil Gains."
"The Year of the Quiet Computer." See "Three Coins in an Enigmatic Fountain."
"Yin, Yang, and Jung." *Vector,* 87 (1978).
"The Young Soldier's Horoscope." In *Orbit 12.* Ed. Damon Knight. New York: Putnams, 1973, pp. 89-113. Incorporated into *The Malacia Tapestry.*

PSEUDONYMOUS STORIES

As Jael Cracken
"The Impossible Star," *Science Fantasy,* May 1965, pp. 5-43; June 1965,

pp. 5–44.

"Lazarus." *Science Fantasy*, June/July 1964, pp. 60–78.

As Peter Pica

Articles for *Brightfount Diaries*. In *The Bookseller*, 1954–1955.

As John Runciman

"No Moon Tonight." *Science Fantasy*, July/August 1964, pp. 92–117.

"Unauthorized Persons." *Science Fantasy*, June/July 1964, pp. 79–112.

As C. C. Shackelton

"Give Me Excess of It, That Something Snaps." *SF Horizons*, 1 (Spring 1964), 58–62.

"How Are They All on Deneb IV." *SF Horizons*, 2 (Winter 1965), 61–63.

"The Serpent of Kundalini." See main index.

"Two Modern Myths" ("Reflection on Mars" and "Ultimate Construction"), *Titbits*, 1967.

V. CRITICISM AND OTHER NON-FICTION: This listing is intended primarily to suggest the scope of Aldiss' non-fiction. It is a checklist and does not attempt to provide a comprehensive bibliography. It does not include, for example, Aldiss' hundreds of book reviews.

Afterwords. The essays concluding a number of Aldiss' anthologies are particularly important in defining his perspectives on science fiction and literature in general, both as author and as critic:

"A Day in the Life-Style of. . . ." In *Best SF: 1971*.

"An Awful Lot of Copy." In *Best SF: 1969*.

"The Day Equality Broke Out." In *Best SF: 1970*.

"Envoi." In *Space Opera*.

"Epilogue." In *Galactic Empires*, Vol. II.

"The Galaxy Begins at Home." In *Best SF: 1974*.

"The House That Jules Built." In *Best SF: 1968*.

"Knights of the Paper Spaceship: A Retrospective Glance at Science Fiction." In *Best SF: 1967*.

Afterword to "The Night That All Time Broke Out." In *Dangerous Visions*. Ed. Harlan Ellison. New York: Doubleday, 1967.

"Science Fiction on the Titanic." In *Best SF: 1975*.

"The Wizard and the Plumber." In *Best SF: 1973*.

"The Year of the Big Spring Clean." In *Best SF: 1972*.

"The Ambidextrous Universe." *Priapus* 21 (Spring 1971). Poetry.

"Anna Kavan: In Memoriam." In *Nebula Award Stories 4*. Ed. Poul Anderson. New York: Doubleday, 1969; London: Gollancz, 1969.

"Barefoot Poems—Living: Being: Having." *Priapus*, 18 (Summer 1969). Poetry.

"'Beyond Apollo' Statement." *Bulletin* (SFWA), 9, no. 2/3 (Summer 1973), 18.

Billion Year Spree. London: Weidenfeld & Nicolson, 1973; New York:

Doubleday, 1973.

"Biography." *Priapus*, 13 (Spring 1968). Poetry.

"Black Monarchy." In *The Saturday Book 27*. Ed. John Hadfield. London: Hutchinson, 1967.

"British Science Fiction Now." *SF Horizons*, 2 (1965), 13-37.

"Chinese Cinema-Owner, Medan." *The Times*, 24 December 1971. Poetry.

Cities and Stones: A Traveller's Yugoslavia. London: Faber, 1966.

"The City in the Sky." *Illustrated London News*, 16 May 1970.

"The Crowded Cities of Patagonia." In *New Worlds Nine*. Ed. Hilary Bailey. London: Corgi, 1975. Drama.

"C. S. Lewis Discusses Science Fiction With Kingsley Amis." *SF Horizons*, 1 (Spring 1964), 5-12. Also published as "The Establishment Must Rot and Die." "Unreal Estates." Discussion between Aldiss, Kingsley Amis, and C. S. Lewis.

"Destruction of the Fifth Planet." *Star*Line* [Science Fiction Poetry Association], March/April 1982, p. 11. Poetry.

"Dick's Maledictory Web: About and Around *Martian Time-Slip*." *Science-Fiction Studies*, March 1975.

Distant Encounters. Play [adaptation of Aldiss' short fictions]; produced in London, 1978.

"A Delicious Circle." In *New Worlds Nine*. Ed. Hilary Bailey. London: Corgi, 1975. Drama.

"Dishonesties of a Lonely Filling Station." In *New Worlds Nine*. Ed. Hilary Bailey. London: Corgi, 1975. Drama.

"The Downward Journey: Orwell's *1984*." *Extrapolation*, 25 (Spring 1984), 5-11.

"E. H. Visiak, 1878-1972." *Bulletin* (SFWA), 8, no. 43 (1972), 6.

"The Empire of Science Fiction." In *SF Symposium*. Ed. Jose Sanz. Instituto National de Cinema, Brazil, 1969. Speech delivered at the Rio de Janeiro SF Symposium, March 1969.

"Excommunication." London: Postcard Partnership, 1975. Postcard.

"Fredric Brown." *Bulletin* (SFWA), July 1972, p. 12.

"The Gothic Imagination." *Queen*, 10 December 1969.

"The Gulf and the Forest: Contemporary SF in Britain." *Fantasy and Science Fiction*, April 1978.

"Gunshot Wounds of Wisdom." *Rio Encounter*, November 1969.

Hell's Cartographers. New York: Harper & Row, 1975. Co-edited with Harry Harrison. Includes Aldiss' "Magic and Bare Boards."

"The Hand in the Jar: Metaphor in Wells and Huxley." *Foundation*, September 1979, pp. 26-41.

"How Brightfounts Was Built." *The Bookseller*, 29 November 1955.

"The Impossible Puppet Show." *In Factions*. Ed. Giles Gordon. Michael Joseph, 1974, pp. 83-106. Drama [incorporated into *New Arrivals, Old Encounters*].

Introductions. Aldiss' introductions to a number of volumes also help define his interests and purposes as editor and critic.

The Airs of Earth.
Best Fantasy Stories.
Best Science Fiction of Brian W. Aldiss.
The Book of Brian Aldiss.
Decade the 1940s.
Evil Earths.
"Foreword to Pamela Zoline's 'The Heat Death of the Universe.'" In *The Mirror of Infinity: A Critic's Anthology of Science Fiction.* Ed. Robert Silverberg. New York: Harper & Row, 1970.
Galactic Empires, Vols. I, II.
Gollancz—Sunday Times Best SF Stories.
Ice, by Anna Kavan. New York: Doubleday, 1970.
Introducing Science Fiction.
More Penguin Science Fiction.
Penguin Science Fiction.
The Penguin Science Fiction Omnibus.

"Robots: Low Voltage Ontological Currents." In *The Mechanical God: Machines in Science Fiction.* Ed. Thomas P. Dunn and Richard Ehrlich. Westport, CT: Greenwood, 1982, pp. 3-9.
Space Odysseys.
Space Opera.
Two Tales and Eight Tomorrows. Ed. Harry Harrison.
Yet More Penguin Science Fiction.
Aldiss also wrote section introductions for *Perilous Planets, All About Venus, Evil Earths, Space Opera,* and other anthologies.
"James Blish (1921-1975)." *Bulletin* (SFWA), October 1975, p. 3.
"James Blish: The Mathematics of Behavior." *Foundation,* 13 (1978), 43-50.
"Judgment at Jonbar." *SF Horizons,* 1 (1964), 13-37.
"Limericks." In *Playboy's Book of Limericks.* Ed. Clifford Christ. New York: Playboy Press, 1972. Poetry.
"The Man Who Invented Inventing the Future." *New Worlds SF,* January 1967.
"Mary Woolstonecraft Shelley." In *Science Fiction Writers.* Ed. E. F. Bleiler. New York: Scribners, 1982, pp. 2-9.
"On Being a Literary Pariah." *Extrapolation,* May 1976, pp. 168-177.
"On Writing Science Fiction." *Authentic Science Fiction,* May 1954, pp. 110-112.
"One That Could Control the Moon: Science Fiction Plain and Coloured." In *International Literary Annual,* III. Ed. Arthur Boyars and Pamela Lyons. London: John Calder, 1961, pp. 176-189.
The Pale Shadow of Science. Seattle, WA: Serconia Press, 1985. Includes: "Preparation for What?," "Long Cut to Burma," "Old Bessie," "Science Fiction's Mother Figure" [Mary Shelley], "The Immanent Will Returns" [Olaf Stapledon], "A Whole New Can of Worms"

[Philip K. Dick], "Peep" [James Blish], "A Transatlantic Harrison, Yippee!" [Harry Harrison], "The Atheist's Tragedy Revisited," "The Pale Shadow of Science," "A Monster for All Seasons," and "Helliconia: How and Why."

"The Plot Sickens." *Impulse,* December 1966, pp. 62-66.

"The Profession of Science Fiction 7: Magic and Bare Boards." *Foundation,* May 1974, pp. 6-30.

"Progression of the Species." *Priapus,* 8 (Spring 1967). Poetry.

"The Sacred Carving." In *New Poems,* 2, 2. Ed. Jonathan price and Geoffrey Hill. Fantasy Press, n.d. Poetry.

Science Fiction Art. New York: Bounty, 1975. Compiled and introduced by BWA. Examines representative illustrations by thirty artists, several comic strips, and major themes in science fiction art, including catastrophes, spaceships, planets, aliens, future cities, girls in science fiction, machines, and robots. Also includes a useful index to science fiction magazines.

Science Fiction as Science Fiction. Frome, Somerset: Bran's Head, 1978.

Science Fiction Quiz. London: Weidenfeld & Nicolson, 1983.

"The Secret of Holman Hunt and the Crude Death Rate." In *New Worlds SF,* January 1970.

"SF Art." In *The Saturday Book* 24. Ed. John Hadfield. New York: Macmillan, 1964, pp. 170-183.

"The SF State." *Algol,* 15, 1 (1977-1978), 43-44.

The Shape of Further Things: Speculations on Change. London: Faber, 1970; New York: Doubleday, 1970.

"Sleep." *Star*Line,* January-February 1983, p. 7. Poetry.

"Smile, Please." *Science Fantasy,* August 1958, pp. 116-118.

"Space Burial." *Fantasy and Science Fiction,* July 1957. Poetry.

"There Are No More Good Stories About Mars." *Fantasy and Science Fiction,* June 1963, p. 127. Poetry.

This World and Nearer Ones: Essays Exploring the Familiar. London: Weidenfeld & Nicolson, 1979; Kent, OH: Kent State University Press, 1981.

"To My Third Child." *Daily Telegraph Magazine,* 27 March 1960. Poetry.

"What Dark Non-Literary Passion." *Science-Fiction Studies,* July 1977, pp. 126ff.

"Within the Reach of Storms." *Bulletin* (SFWA), August 1967, pp. 9-14.

"The Wounded Land: J. G. Ballard." *SF Horizons,* 2 (1965), 26-37; also in *SF: The Other Side of Realism.* Ed. Thomas Clareson. Bowling Green, OH: Bowling Green University Press, 1971.

CO-AUTHORED ARTICLES

With Kingsley Amis and C. S. Lewis, "The Establishment Must Die and Rot. . . ." *SF Horizons,* 1 (1964), 5-12.

With Jon Bing and John-Henri Holmberg, "Science Fiction and Politics."

In *Volve: Scandinavian Views on Science Fiction.* Ed. Cay Dollerup. Copenhagen: University of Copenhagen, 1978, pp. 66–69.

With Richard Cooper and Thomas M. Disch, *"Foundations* Forum: Problems in Creativeness." *Foundation,* May 1978, pp. 65–73.

With Harry Harrison, "Other Critical Works." *SF Horizons,* 2 (1965), 48–50.

Notes

I am indebted to Margaret Aldiss' *Item 83* (1972) and Griffin and Wingrove's bibliography in *Apertures* for many items in this checklist. Mrs. Aldiss also made a number of additions to my original draft for this chapter, drawing on her own extensive bibliography of Aldiss' works.

This list does not include titles for short fiction readily available in Aldiss' collections; stories from *Foreign Bodies,* are included, for example, because that volume is highly inaccessible.

XV

Selectively Annotated Secondary Bibliography:
A Checklist of Criticism

Adlard, Mark. "Billion Year Spree: A Labour of Love." *Foundation*, May 1974, pp. 61–69.

Aldiss, Margaret. *Item Eighty-Three: Brian Aldiss: A Bibliography, 1954–1972*. Southmoor, England: SF Horizons, 1972. A valuable bibliographic reference to Aldiss' works to 1972.

Ash, Brian. *The Visual Encyclopedia of Science Fiction*. London: Pan, 1977; New York: Harmony, 1977.

–––––. *Who's Who in Science Fiction*. London: Hamilton, 1976; New York: Taplinger, 1976, 32–33.

Ashley, Mike, ed. *The Illustrated Book of Science Fiction Lists*. London: Virgin Books, 1982, 97. Aldiss listed as ninth most prolific short story writer.

Atheling, William, Jr. (James Blish). *More Issues at Hand*. Chicago: Advent, 1964.

Barron, Neil. Entries in *Anatomy of Wonder: Science Fiction*. New York: R. R. Bowker, 1976; 2 ed, 1981.

Bengtson, Goran. *"Billion Year Spree*–an Open Letter." *Foundation*, May 1974, pp. 69–73.

Blish, James. "Is This Thinking?" *SF Horizons*, 1 (1964), 54–57. Discusses Aldiss' poetic and romantic approach to science fiction.

Bower, Bill, and Bill Maladri, eds. Replies to Lloyd Biggle's Questionnaire in *The Double Bill Symposium*. Akron, OH, September 1979.

Brunner, John. "The Genesis of *Stand on Zanzibar* and Digressions into the Remainder of its Pentateuch." *Extrapolation*, May 1970, pp. 34–43.

Buckley, Kathryn (Pamela Bulmer). Review of *Barefoot in the Head*. In *Vision of Tomorrow*, March 1970.

Clareson, Thomas D. *Science Fiction Criticism: An Annotated Checklist*. Kent, OH: Kent State University Press, 1972.

Colbert, Robert E. "Unbinding Frankenstein: The Science Fiction Criticism of Brian Aldiss." *Extrapolation*, 23, no. 4 (Winter 1982), 333–344. Draws on *BYS* and Aldiss' critical afterwords in the *Best SF* series to define Aldiss' critical assumptions.

Collings, Michael R. "Brian W. Aldiss: Cartographer." Presented to the International Conference on the Fantastic in the Arts. Boca Raton, FL, March 1984.

—————. "Brothers of the Head: Brian W. Aldiss' Psychological Landscape." Presented to the International Conference on the Fantastic in the Arts. Beaumont, TX, March 1985.

—————. Review of *Apertures: A Study of the Writings of Brian W. Aldiss*, by Brian Griffin and David Wingrove. *Fantasy Review*, April 1984, p. 35.

—————. Review of *Life in the West. Fantasy Review*, May 1984, p. 24.

Crispin, Edmund, "Brian Aldiss: The Image Maker." *New Worlds SF*, September 1965, pp. 3–11.

Dunn, Thomas P. and Richard P. Ehrlich, eds. "List of Works Useful for the Study of Machines in Science Fiction." In *The Mechanical God: Machines in Science Fiction*. Westport, CT: Greenwood, 1982, pp. 231-232.

Gillespie, Bruce. "Literature Which Awakens Us: The Science Fiction Novels of Brian W. Aldiss." In *Stellar Gauge: Essays on Modern Science Fiction Writers*. Ed. Michael J. Tolley and Kirpal Singh. Melbourne, Australia: Norstrilia, 1980, pp. 153-185. Excellent study of Aldiss' *ouevre* through *Frankenstein Unbound*.

—————. "Sentio Ergo Sum." *SF Commentary*, March–April 1970. Discussions of *Equator, Non-Stop, The Male Response, Hothouse*, and *Greybeard*.

—————. "The SF Novels of Brian W. Aldiss, Part I: 'The Great Adventurer,'" *SF Commentary*, April 1972, pp. 67-68.

—————. "The SF Novels of Brian W. Aldiss, Part II: 'Poor Little Warriors,'" *SF Commentary*, August 1972, pp. 25-42, 48.

Greenland, Colin. "The Works of Brian Aldiss." In *The Entropy Exhibition: Michael Moorcock and the British 'New Wave' in Science Fiction*. London: Routledge & Kegan Paul, 1983, pp. 64-92. Concentrates on *RPA* and *Barefoot*; includes a brief primary bibliography.

—————. "The Times Themselves Talk Nonsense: Language in *Barefoot in the Head*." *Extrapolation*, 17 (1979), 32-41.

Griffin, Brian, and David Wingrove. *Apertures: A Study of the Writings of Brian W. Aldiss*. Contributions to the Study of Science Fiction and Fantasy, No. 8 Westport, CT: Greenwood, 1984. The first full-length treatment of Aldiss; focuses on his relationship with mainstream fiction. Includes an extensive primary bibliography.

Hodgens, Richard. "Book Notes." *Bulletin of the New York C. S. Lewis Society*, 7, no. 3 (1976), 8-12.

Holmes, H. H. "Science and Fantasy." *New York Herald Tribune Book Review*, 20 September 1959, 15.

Jameson, Fredric. "Generic Discontinuity in SF: Brian Aldiss' *Starship*." *Science-Fiction Studies*, 1, no. 2 (1973), 57-68. Seminal discussion of Aldiss' first novel.

Ketterer, David. *New Worlds for Old: The Apocalyptic Imagination. Science Fiction, and American Literature*. Bloomington, IN: University of Indiana Press, 1974, pp. vi, ix, 125-26, 139, 204, 235, 255-60.

McNelly, Willis E. "Brian W. Aldiss." In *Science Fiction Writers.* Ed. E. F. Bleiler. New York: Scribners, 1982, pp. 251-258. Bio-critical introduction to Aldiss and his novels through *Helliconia*; includes a brief bibliography of major books.

McLeod, Patrick. "Frankenstein: Unbound and Otherwise." *Extrapolation*, 21, no. 2 (1981), 158-166. Some discussion of Shelley, but primarily a critical assessment of Aldiss.

Magill, Frank N., ed. *Survey of Science Fiction Literature.* Englewood Cliffs, NJ: Salem Press, 1979. Vols. 1-5. Includes: Grace Eckley, *"Barefoot in the Head."* I, pp. 125-29; Bruce Gillespie, *"Cryptozoic!."* I, pp. 443-48; Willis E. McNelly, *"Frankenstein Unbound."* II, pp. 840-44; Bruce Gillespie, *"Greybeard."* II, pp. 926-31; Harry Harrison, *"Long Afternoon of Earth."* III, pp. 1235-37; Willis E. McNelly, *"Report on Probability A."* IV, pp. 1764-67.

Manson, Margaret. *Item Forty-Three: Brian W. Aldiss: A Bibliography, 1954-1962.* Birmingham: Dryden Press, 1962. An early version of *Item Eighty-Three.*

Mathews, Richard. *Aldiss Unbound: The Science Fiction of Brian W. Aldiss.* Milford Series: Popular Writers of Today, Vol. 9. San Bernardino, CA: Borgo, 1977. The best and most accessible introduction to Aldiss; critical statements on his writings through *MT* and *Last Orders.* Brief primary bibliography, restricted to published volumes.

Milicia, Joseph. Introduction to *Hothouse.* New York: Baen, 1984, pp. 1-18. (Paperback rpt of G. K. Hall, 1976 ed.). A critical assessment of *Hothouse,* including discussion of differences between the texts of the original novel and the American reprint, *Long Afternoon of Earth.*

Nicholls, Peter, ed. "Brian Aldiss." In *The Science Fiction Encyclopedia.* London: Granada, 1979; New York: Doubleday, 1979, pp. 19-21.

Ozolina, Aija. "Recent Work on Mary Shelley and *Frankenstein." Science-Fiction Studies,* 3 (1976), pp. 187-202, esp. 198-199.

Parrinder, Patrick. *Science Fiction: Its Criticism and Teaching.* London: Methuen, 1980, pp. 18-19, 24-27. Discussions of *BYS* and *MT.*

Platt, Charles, ed. *Who Writes Science Fiction?* London: Savoy, 1980; as *Dream Makers,* New York: Berkley, 1980, pp. 297-309.

Pringle, David. "Time Must Have a Stop." *Extrapolation,* March 1977, pp. 93-96. Review article on *MT.*

Smith, Curtis C., ed. "Brian Aldiss." In *Twentieth-Century Science-Fiction Writers.* London: Macmillan, 1981, pp. 11-13.

Spenser, William. "Brian Aldiss Futurologist." *Penthouse,* August 1971, pp. 28-32.

Storm, Jannick. "Mennesket i rummet: Brian W. Aldiss' *Outside of Science Fiction."* In *Meddeleser fra Dansklaererforeningen* (1971), pp. 306-314.

——————. *Vor tids eventyr: Katastrofeomradet: Udvalqte science fiction rapporter 1963-1977.* Ed. Turrell. Copenhagen: Swing, 1978.

Swahn, Sven Christer. *7 x framtiden.* Oslo: Bernces, 1974, pp. 89-122.

Tuck, Donald M., ed. "Brian W. Aldiss." In *The Encyclopedia of Science Fiction and Fantasy,* Vol. I: Who's Who A-L. Chicago: Advent, 1974, pp. 3-5.

Tymn, Marshall. *The Science Fiction Reference Book.* Mercer Island, WA: Starmont, 1981. Multiple references to Aldiss.

—————— and Roger Schlobin. Entries in *The Year's Scholarship in Science Fiction and Fantasy.* Kent, OH: Kent State University, 1972-1975.

Versins, Pierre, ed. Entry in *Encyclopedie de l'Utopie et de la Science Fiction.* Lausanne: l'Age de l'Homme, 1972, pp. 24-25.

White, Peter. "Brian Aldiss." *New Worlds SF,* September 1965, p. 118.

Wilson, Colin. "The Vision of Science." In *The Strength to Dream: Literature and the Imagination.* London: Gollancz, 1962, pp. 94-127. Esp. pp. 120-121, a discussion of Aldiss' short story "Outside."

Wingrove, David. "Thinking in Fuzzy Sets: The Recent SF of Brian W. Aldiss." *Pacific Quarterly* (Moana), 4 (1979), pp. 288-294.

In addition to the works cited above, there are many valuable individual reviews of Aldiss' works, as well as other critical articles and references to Aldiss in general studies of contemporary science fiction.

Aldiss also appears in the following indices:

Bogart, Gary L. *Short Story Index, 1981.* New York: H. W. Wilson, 1982, 4. See other annual issues.

Contento, William, ed. *Index to Science Fiction Anthologies and Collections.* Boston: G. K. Hall, 1978, pp. 29-32.

Curry, L. W., ed. *Science Fiction and Fantasy Authors: A Bibliography of First Printings of their Fictions.* Boston: G. K. Hall, 1979, pp. 1-8.

Day, Bradford M., ed. *The Complete Checklist of Science-Fiction Magazines.* New York, 1961.

Fletcher, Marilyn R., ed. *Science Fiction Story Index, 1950-1979.* 2nd ed. Chicago: American Library Association, 1981, pp. 1, 297-301.

Index to the Science-Fiction Magazines, 1966-1970. West Hanover, MA: New England Science Fiction Association, 1971.

Index to Science Fiction Magazines and Original Anthologies, 1971-1976.

Reginald, R., ed. *Science Fiction and Fantasy Literature: A Checklist, 1700-1974.* Vol. I, pp. 8-9; Vol. II, pp. 792-793. Detroit: Gale Research, 1979.

Rock, James A., comp. *Who Goes There: A Bibliographical Dictionary.* Bloomington, IN: J. A. Rock, 1979.

Simeon, Frederick, comp. *Science Fiction Story Index, 1950-1968.* Chicago: American Library Association, 1971, pp. 2-3.

Straus, Erwin R., comp. *Index to the S-F Magazines, 1951-1965.* Cambridge, MA: MIT Science Fiction Society, 1966.

Tymn, Marshall, and others, eds. *Index to Stories in Thematic Antholo-*

gies of Science Fiction. Boston: G. K. Hall, 1978.

Wells, Stuart W., III. *The Science Fiction and Heroic Fantasy Author Index.* Duluth, MN: Purple Unicorn, 1978.

INDEX
A Selective Index of Names and Titles.

112

PR 6051 .L3 Z6 1986

Collins, Michael R.

Brian Aldiss

PR 6051 .L3 Z6 1986

Collins, Michael R.

Brian Aldiss

HAMMERMILL LIBRARY

MAY 2 1 1987